AF443477

COME, JOIN THE FAMILY

COME, JOIN THE FAMILY

Barry Bailey

ABINGDON PRESS
NASHVILLE

COME, JOIN THE FAMILY

Library of Congress Cataloging-in-Publication Data
Bailey, Barry, 1926-
   Come join the family.

   1. Christian life—1960-   . 2. Christianity—20th century.
I. Title.
BV4501.2.B276   1986   248.4   86-8056

ISBN 0-687-08880-1 (alk. paper)

All scripture quotations are the author's paraphrases.

MANUFACTURED BY THE PARTHENON PRESS AT
NASHVILLE, TENNESSEE, UNITED STATES OF AMERICA

Contents

Come, Join the Family

1

W*here Is Home?*

Scripture: Exodus 2:7-10

We have so many preconceived ideas about motherhood and the home. For many of us, these ideas are deeply rooted. If possible, let's free ourselves of some of these presuppositions and give ourselves the liberty to consider some thoughts.

We might begin with Moses. He certainly did not have what we would term an average childhood. He was born a Hebrew in a country where the Hebrew people were enslaved by the Egyptians; moreover, the male Hebrew children were being killed. His mother however was resourceful. In order to protect him, she kept him hidden at home for three months after his birth. Then she had an idea. She would take a chance; what did she have to lose? She made a little boat, rather like a bassinet, that would float. She told her daughter, Miriam, to take it out to the water and put it close to the shore where Pharaoh's daughter came to bathe. After doing this, Miriam was to hide and observe what happened. When the baby was found, Moses' mother reasoned, in all probability Pharaoh's daughter would love the child.

Perhaps Moses' mother understood that we can hate generally, that we can kill all the babies on a wholesale basis. But can we do that after we have looked a child in the face? Hatred is different when it's personified. We can imagine someone so filled with racial hatred, some Caucasian who detests all other races and ethnic groups. He is filled with hate, and he justifies it because he thinks he is so pure. He thinks, "God must be white; Jesus must be white; I'm white. Everything good is white. Sin is dark, truth is light." But I would imagine, unless this person's mind is totally demented, that while he may hate the blacks in general, surely if he saw firsthand one black baby or one individual, if he really saw this person, he might begin to think, "We are alike, are we not? We feel; we crave the same things; we need the same things."

When Pharaoh's daughter came to bathe, she saw the basket and sent her maid out to retrieve it. When she opened it she saw the child. "It's a Hebrew child," she said. At that point, Miriam, Moses' sister, emerged from her hiding place and asked, "Do you want me to find a nurse for you among the Hebrew women?" When Pharaoh's daughter said yes, Miriam brought her own mother, the mother of Moses. Now Pharaoh's daughter said, "Take this child and nurse him for me, and I will pay you." That's exactly what Moses' mother did. She nursed him and taught him. One day she brought him back to Pharaoh's daughter to remain with her as her son, but Moses' mother had taught him to know that he was a Hebrew, that he had a purpose.

Meanwhile, he stayed with the Pharaoh's daughter in security, splendor, and comfort.

After he was grown, and a prince, he saw two people fighting, a Hebrew and an Egyptian. He hit the Egyptian, killing him, and then Moses had to flee for his own life to the desert of Sinai, where he lived for a considerable time. Later, he was married and lived in safety and security. His father-in-law, apparently, was quite wealthy. Moses could have stayed in the land of Midian forever. However, one day he saw a bush burning and it was not consumed by the fire. From within the bush, he heard a voice of God telling him to go back to Egypt and lead his people out of slavery.

It seems to me this event would have had no meaning if his mother had not taught him. To what are we going to connect this event? A bush is burning—what does this mean? Nothing, absolutely nothing. We can diminish almost any kind of spiritual experience if we want to; it has no meaning unless we harness it. Moses however remembered who he was; he remembered the woman who taught him.

There had been nothing normal about his childhood. He had had to be hidden in order to save his life. He was raised by his own mother as a foster son, and then given to a foster mother as her son. He grew up as an Egyptian when he was a Hebrew. Think of the confusion. Yet he knew who he was. He went back to Egypt in order to do that which he felt was right in his own soul. The Hebrews were slaves, and he led them out of Egypt.

Where was home for Moses? Egypt? The encampment at the Red Sea? The wilderness? Nowhere. Home was a moving relationship. And so it always is.

The present day is a period of change, quite obviously. The church needs to look at people who are single. We do not use the term "Family Night" in our church. But once a month, at least six or seven months of the year, we have what is called "Church Nite." Although *family* is a marvelous word, I didn't want to apply it to these nights, because sometimes one needs to convey what is really meant. So often, people think of *family* as being a husband and a wife; father, mother, and children. What about someone living alone? Why, that person is a part of our family, of course. We use the words "Church Nite" to bring all of us together.

Singleness. The largest church-school class in our church, numerically speaking, is a singles' class. In fact, we have a number of singles' classes. For years the church didn't know how to handle singles because the culturally accepted idea was that one married and stayed married. That was the total thrust of life. A woman was born into the world and her sole purpose was to grow up, marry, and have children. That's marvelous. There is nothing in the world wrong with that except for the fact that, due to a number of circumstances, many people now are not allowed or choose not to live that way. There are people who love and do not marry; there are those who have married and then divorced. Some would like to have the right job, to make a certain amount of money, to have someone to love who loves them. But sometimes that just does not happen. If the church is only going to deal with that which is predictable and that which makes us feel comfortable, we either ought to get out of the business or simply rock the cradle.

I hope that people who are single can also hear the word *health*. In America, are we not in danger of making a little god out of the family? There are movements today claiming that the family is the most important thing in our country. I don't believe that. The most important thing in America is people. A family is sacred because the person is sacred. You don't become sacred just because you are part of what is known as a conventional family. Home is fixed but it is also moving. This was true in Moses' life, and it was true in the life of Jesus.

There are people who do not have children. Should a woman feel her life has been invalidated because she does not have children? For many years, the church has almost said, in effect, "You owe it to us to have as many children as possible. The church wants to be strong and vibrant. We want to be dominant in the world; therefore, we want to grow as many Christians as possible." Some of that attitude arises from the Old Testament. We see it demonstrated in the lives of Abraham and Sarah. Sarah didn't have a child, so she told her husband, Abraham, "Since this is embarrassing to me, go and be with my handmaiden, Hagar. If she conceives, then her child will be as mine." I don't believe that the main purpose of a woman's life is to marry and have children. Yet we have made women feel guilty with that message for far too long.

Society has helped to manipulate the role of women. We are rarely much better than our society or much better than our environment. If we had lived in Germany at the time of Hitler, we couldn't have been much better than that society. Occasionally, someone may think thoughts that are way beyond the general trends of thought, but most of us are mentally part of those around us. And so it is today. From some religious points of view around the world, the thought is that women are supposed to produce children. If you don't have a child, it is still believed by some that God has something against you. You wonder if you have committed a sin, if it is a punishment. The birth of a child can be a marvelous experience, but it is not the criterion of your validity and worth as a woman.

Yet, to a great extent, by taking a stance against birth control and birth control information, the church has said that God, in his mind, expects women to produce children and something is wrong if they do not. Don't you long, at times, for the church to grow up and do what it obviously ought to do, which is to have some sense, some good judgment, undergirded by love? Wouldn't you like to move out to where God may be trying to lead us, rather than clinging to our culture, haloing it, and saying, "This is of God"?

Divorce. Today, there are multitudes of people who are divorced. A divorce is like death; it's a form of hell. I have never known anyone who wanted to go through a divorce even though, at times, it might have been unbearable to stay married. Some time ago, someone said to me, "When you go through a divorce you are so utterly alone, particularly if you are a woman, because so often you lose your close friends. They can be afraid of you. When someone dies, people come to the house. They are there, and they talk about it openly. But when there's a divorce, it's almost as if your friends are embarrassed to discuss it, so they talk about other things. They go to great lengths to avoid what is breaking your heart." Of course, we want a marriage to be sacred and secure, but the church is in the redemptive world of dealing with people.

Today, any open discussion of the home must include some reference to child abuse. Imagine the children who have to relearn the idea of honoring their fathers and mothers because they have been battered and bruised for so long. They have been physically, verbally, spiritually, and emotionally scarred by the people they are closer to than anyone else in the world. In such circumstances, it's frightening if you talk about God being a father. There are parents who are so ill that they almost destroy their children. What do children think in such a family? "I know my mother loves me; I know my father loves me. I guess a beating is love." The last thing children usually recognize is the fact that their parent or parents really don't want them, that their parents are ill. The child who does reach that point quickly, however, may be able to get out of the situation or be rescued by someone. Such children can also leave home when they are older. But usually they continue to think, "I know they love me. I hear people talking about parents. They must love me; they brought me into the world. They love me." Many battered children are confused about what love is.

Motherhood is important; it is vital. But, in the name of God, should we not deal with it in a realistic way? There is nothing we need more in this world of ours than that which is personified by motherhood at its best. We are in dire need of the redemptive quality of love, the love that comes to us without waiting for us to deserve it or to ask for it. We need the love that does not wait for anything, but is just simply there.

While child abuse is a horrible problem that we must try to eradicate, we should also recognize that normal homes need help, too. Most of us probably live in rather average homes, yet we need all the help we can get just because of the give and take of life. Some time ago I was talking with my mother and she told me about an experience she had had with one of our relatives. A few years after my father died, when my mother was visiting with this relative and some other people, someone happened to mention my father's death and, for some reason, also mentioned the fact that my mother had been very concerned about selecting a certain casket. This relative, who always finds a way to be very critical, spoke up and said, "Well, it won't last." My mother said, "What do you mean?"

"Why," the relative said, "the casket won't last." Mother said, "I hadn't thought of that; I suppose not."

"I just wanted to tell you, Marguerite," the relative continued, "it won't last."

Everyone has someone like that in their family—and they never miss a family reunion! We need all the help we can get!

Usually mothers long to try to help their children. That's true whether your mother is someone you really love or not, or whether or not she is ill. I think you can rely on this, even though it may not be obvious. We all have wanted to help people when we were not able to do so. We meant well, but perhaps the end result was not what we would wish. We all make mistakes and, along with that, we intentionally sin at times.

Former president Jimmy Carter spoke at Southern Methodist University recently. He related an incident that occurred after he left the White House. A woman reporter came to Plains, Georgia, to interview his mother in relation to an article about Mr. Carter and his family. His mother really didn't want to be interviewed, but was being gracious. So when the reporter knocked at her door, Mrs. Carter invited her in. The reporter asked some hard questions and actually was rather aggressive and rude.

"I want to ask you a question. Your son ran for the presidency on the premise that he would always tell the truth. Has he ever lied?"

Mrs. Carter said, "I think he's truthful; I think you can depend upon his word."

The reporter again asked if he had ever lied in his entire life.

His mother said, "Well, I guess maybe he's told a little white lie."

"Ah, see there!" the reporter exclaimed. "He's lied! If he told a white lie, he has lied. What is a white lie?"

And then Lillian Carter said, "It's like a moment ago when you knocked on the door and I went to the door and said I was glad to see you."

Moses was taught by his mother. What happened when that bush was burning? I don't know. Perhaps it was no more than the rays of the sun hitting a bush and making it red so that it seemed to be in flames. But I can tell you, something powerful happened that involved not the bush so much as Moses' life. That's the power.

If you want to call it a miracle, let the miracle be there. Moses remembered what his mother had taught him. He was a Hebrew and his people were back in Egypt as slaves.

Moses remembered what his mother had taught him and we should, too. If you go back in your mind and begin to think about growing up, you recall all kinds of experiences. You laugh and you cry, you experience disappointment and joy. That "ought" within you, you were taught; you know what you ought to do. That is not restrictive or too confining; it doesn't give you claustrophobia. It's the quality of caring; it's the standards, the principles. You have high standards. You make mistakes, and you give yourself the latitude to forgive yourself and other people.

Finally, while a mother's influence is important, we find our true strength in God. Our strength cannot come just from a woman, our mother, or from a man, our father, or from our own selves, regardless of how talented, wealthy, or lucky we are. I hope we realize this voluntarily before it is forced upon us. Let us go on and get ready; invite people into our lives, get love in our lives. Let's not wait until something disastrous happens and we find we are absolutely truncated. God is the source of our strength.

Some time ago I read a very personal statement by Truman Capote, the brilliant writer who, at times, was terribly confused. He could write with such clarity, and then his psyche could become so foggy. He probably personified the extremes that can be found in personalities. He wrote this statement when he was very disappointed. Actually, it is a conversation he had with his alter ego, what he called his "Siamese twin."

As he tries to get some sleep, he talks to his Siamese twin. "But first let's say a prayer," he tells himself. "The one we used to say when we were growing up and our dog, Queenie, used to sleep with us. We would get under the quilts and pull them up over our heads because the house was so big and cold. . . . 'Now I lay me down to sleep, I pray the Lord my soul to keep. And if I should die before I wake, I pray the Lord my soul to take. Amen.' "

And then he bids himself goodnight. "I love you," he says. "I love you, too," he answers. And then he says, "You'd better. Because when you get right down to it, all we've got is each other. Alone. To the grave. And that's the tragedy, isn't it?"

"You forget," he answers. "We have God, too."

That says it; that's exactly right. You have yourself; you are wedded to yourself. From one point of view, that's all you have. You have memories, relationships, and people who love you; you have been taught remarkably well. But that's not all you have. You have God, too.

Your home is fixed; you know the address; you know it quite well. You can picture it in your mind. But your home really is a moving goal. It's a direction; it's a quality.

"Moses, where is your home? Egypt?" So he had to go back, didn't he?

Was that his home? No, not really. Where was his home? It was in his heart, in the mind of his mother, in the mind of God.

Home is that quality in you that God takes when he calls you to contribute to life, to grow and develop, and to become, under God, what only you should be.

2

Come, Join the Family

Scripture: Luke 15:11-32

Each one of us, at some time in our life, has felt victimized. We have felt that we were treated unfairly, that we were short-changed. What happens when you feel cheated? To begin to answer that question, let's look at the story of the prodigal son.

A landowner had two sons. The younger son turned to his father and said, "Give me what is mine." After his father complied with his request, the son left home and wasted what he had been given. Later, he wanted to return home. He felt the best he could hope for was to be accepted as a servant, but his father welcomed him as a son.

This is a marvelous story; it is the greatest story I know of in the Bible. Many people might say that it is one of the greatest stories in all of literature. It is teaching at its best. Jesus tells us a parable from which we may take what meaning we can.

A portion of the story reads, "But when he was yet a great way off, his father saw him, and had compassion, and ran, and fell on his neck, and kissed him."

No wonder! The father thought his son would never come home again. The father killed a fatted calf. He put shoes on his son's feet, a robe on his back, a ring on his finger, and said, "This my son was dead, and is alive again; he was lost, and is found." How could you improve on that?

Have you had a similar experience in your life? We may not have had the experience of going to a far country like the prodigal son, but most of us know what it is to have a strained, broken relationship. Those are times when things are not going well for us; we feel awkward, embarrassed, left out. We have been estranged. Then we come back, not expecting anything very good, and not asking for much. But the unbelievable happens—we are accepted in the same way we were before we left. That's love! That's mercy!

When you read this story literally, the elder brother appears in a negative light. Yet you and I need to see ourselves in the elder brother, or sister, as much as in the prodigal son.

In the story the father realized that his family was still not together; one son had returned, but he had lost the other. So the father went out into the yard and talked with the elder brother. The elder brother said very clearly, "As soon as your son [not "my brother"] came home, you killed the fatted calf. You've never given me a kid."

His father reasoned with him, saying, "Everything I have is yours. You've been with me all this time."

Nonetheless, we can imagine what the elder brother was thinking: "I saw you *run* down the road to meet him. You only walked out here to see me. I know I own the flocks; I could go get my own kid or a calf for a feast.'' In a sense, this implies that the father has retired and the elder brother is running the farm. "I'm doing just what I'm supposed to do, but don't you think I have feelings, too? Do you really see me as just a part of the atmosphere? You ran to him; you walked to me. I've been here so long you've overlooked me. I'm not talking about a calf, a kid, or your son, my brother. What I am talking about is, do you care about me?"

There comes a time when it is possible to deprive one family member if you are very generous to another. In terms of mercy, in dealing with the intangible, we can give love however much and it increases. We can give compassion however much and it multiplies. But the moment we start dealing with material possessions, we are not merciful if we are not just. If we try to be inordinately generous to one child in our family, what are we doing? We are taking from someone else. Granted, there are times when one's need may exceed another's. In that case, we need to explain it to both parties; then our generosity may vary and still be just.

We need to understand that mercy without justice can be destructive. For so long we have preached in the church that God in his mercy has chosen the Christian. Do we really think that? Or, we have preached that God in his mercy has chosen the Christian and the Jew over everyone else. Do we really believe that? Then, what kind of a God do we have? There is really no mercy unless there is also justice.

While we are considering justice, I think we need to

recognize that life is not fair. We don't all start at the same place. It's been said that everybody is equal to everybody else, but some are more equal than others. We certainly know that this is true. Where is there equality? I think our country's judicial system is the best system there is. But do you honestly believe that there is always parity in the courts? Do you really think a black person always has the same chance as a white person? Or, sometimes a black person may have an advantage, depending upon the circumstances. Ethnic background can make a difference. We are not totally objective, are we?

Nor is there intellectual equivalence. There may be one school child who can just come to class and learn, almost by osmosis. One wonders how he or she can be so bright with so little effort, and make almost straight A's. And then there may be another student who really tries, who expends every effort, but simply cannot master the material.

A few years ago, a friend of mine told me about one of his friends who had failed medical school. He said, "Barry, I didn't know of anyone who loved medicine more than he did. I think he would have made a good doctor, but he just couldn't do the work fast enough. It wasn't that he wasn't sharp. He could really retain whatever he learned, but he just couldn't go fast enough."

We are not all equal in everything, and life is not totally fair. Sometimes we try to equalize these imbalances in terms of faith. We say, in effect, "God will make up to you later what you don't get here." We particularly say that to the "have nots" when we are the "haves." "Be spiritual and you will get heaven when you die." That's what we used to say to the blacks on the plantations: "Hoe the cotton, and when you die you'll get to go to heaven." The promise of a heavenly reward can be the equalizer in terms of faith.

At a recent meeting of the General Conference of The United Methodist Church, I served on a committee called Church and Society, which dealt with various social issues. Someone made a proposal, which passed, that we be particularly sensitive to older women and minorities. It seemed to me they were excluding one group, so I raised my hand and asked, "What about older men?" That wasn't a good question to ask at that time.

The woman who made the proposal said, "Well, let's face it; men have more money than women." I thought, "Honey, you haven't checked lately." She also said that men fared better in the economic market. I do agree with that, because men, by and large, are paid better than women for the same jobs. And she said, older women have been neglected for so long that we need to assist them. I agreed with that, and that we should be sensitive to minorities; but I still wanted to know about the older men. Almost in exasperation, she turned to me and said, "First of all, men usually have the money."

"I doubt that," I said, "but go ahead."

And then she said, "Besides, men die." Well, that took care of it. They don't live as long as women, so that really settles the problem, doesn't it? That was supposed to answer the question. I said, "What about an older man who doesn't die and doesn't have much money? He really is in the minority."

We try to be just. We want to be fair. But some of our efforts are so silly! What was our committee really trying to say by accepting this proposal? I suppose they were trying to say, "Let us be sensitive to people in need." But look at the parochial way in which we did it.

There is always a conflict between justice and mercy. We may dispense mercy to someone, but often it is at the expense of somebody else. Jesus knew this, and perhaps that is one of the reasons he told the story of the prodigal son. It's not just about the prodigal son coming home, it is also about the elder brother who stayed home. They both have integrity; they both have needs. At times in your life you are the elder brother or sister, at other times you are the younger brother or sister.

When his father came out into the yard to talk to him the elder brother began to say, in effect, "What bothers me is that today I saw you happy for the first time in so long. But I've been here all the time. I didn't expect you to rejoice whenever I came home. You expected me to be here, and I was here. I'm part of the scenery. This is my job. But don't you know I am like he is, too? I didn't have to stay."

It's the elder brother who brings up the subject of harlots. "But when this son of yours came, who has devoured your living with harlots, you killed for him the fatted calf!" I can imagine there was a time when the elder son thought, "I would like to be in the far country, too." All kinds of things must have been going on in his mind. What he was saying was, "I am a person; I'm good, I'm dependable. I have to sacrifice, too. I haven't seen you happy since he's been gone. I can understand that; you love both of us. But you ran down the road, and you welcomed him back. You walked out here in the yard and told me very clearly, 'All I have is yours.' Well, I am not talking about what you have, I'm talking about you. I can go get a kid or a calf, and I can have my own party. But I'm not talking about things."

Here is teaching at its best. This is what the elder brother is arguing here and Jesus has him do it, against his father. "You never gave me a kid. I want to know, will you give me yourself? Do you care about me?"

Unless we have justice, mercy becomes very, very destructive to a lot of people. That is certainly true in our society, where we deal with such complicated issues. I suppose it would be next to impossible for someone to preach today, someone knowledgeable of sociology, who is not concerned about child abuse. In our own church, we have committees studying and working in this area. Child abuse is one of the most horrible facts of life today. A child hasn't learned how to recognize a healthy environment, and a child is abused, most often by the family. That is certainly sick.

I'm the kind of person who gets involved. If I think a child is being abused, I personally try to do something, as many of you do, to try to prevent it. When we at the church learn of a case, we try to get the child out of the house, to do all we can to help. However, having said that, I am afraid it is possible also to develop witch hunts if we are not careful. At times, our response to child abuse almost reminds me of the McCarthy era, when under Senator Joe McCarthy we thought we were finding a Communist under every bush. Check the records if you do not believe this to be true. The number of arrests for child abuse has increased dramatically. Maybe this is called for; perhaps parents are abusing their children more than ever and we have just become sensitive to it. That may be true. But let us be reasonable, sound, and thoughtful. There is a possibility that we are overreacting.

A man is imprisoned because he is supposed to have molested his four or five-year-old son. The child meets with a social worker who means well. They discuss this, and the child's answers vary. They draw pictures, and the child identifies things his father did to him. His mother claims it's not true, that somebody prompted the child because he doesn't think that way. Maybe the mother doesn't know the child as well as she thought she did. There are all kinds of maybes. But, let's face it, the court will never know the truth either. A child that age isn't always able to differentiate between reality and unreality. If the child is not marred physically, we don't really know all that much, do we? Maybe he has been hurt psychologically. Perhaps so, but there is more to it than just someone saying, "The child told me so."

I know of men and women who would be reluctant to pick up a child on the street and give the child a ride home because someone could ask, "Did the person hug you? Did the person touch you?" Well, probably so, but everything you do is sick to a sick mind. We can have close relationships with people, with children, that have no sexual overtones whatsoever. We have become sick if we cannot.

Of course we want to get the children out of an abusive home. We want to help the family recover, and try to get them back together. We want all of that. But every time I read a newspaper article concerning someone who has been accused and convicted, someone we know is guilty, I doubt if we are always that accurate. I wonder if sometimes the person who is questioning the child is dealing with personal problems of his or her own to some degree; maybe they've been hurt, too.

Justice. Of course we want mercy for the children. But justice—what is the fair, honest thing to do? I am trying to say that unless you and I are very circumspect, our mercy can become destructive.

Let's personalize this idea. What if mercy does become destructive and you feel victimized, what should you do? Although it seems rather elementary, it is important—first of all, when it happens to you—to realize that you may have been cheated. Now, there are people who like to think they have been cheated and I'm not referring to them. There was a man who counted his change five times. The cashier asked, "Isn't it right?" And he said, "Yes, but just barely!" I'm not discussing that kind of person. I'm talking about real problems, when you are genuinely ripped off, when you do not get what you deserve, when you are not treated fairly. That happens to every last one of us at one time or another. I've never found anybody who always won. Did Jesus ever win? You recognize your life and I'll recognize mine; there are times when life is just not fair. That's simply how it is.

However, religion can help. I don't use the word *spiritual* often, although I believe in the spiritual very much. To me, *spiritual* is a word that should be used selectively. It is a powerful, significant word. I don't know how you have a healing between people unless it's a spiritual healing.

Notice how Jesus told this story. The younger son was a great way off when the father ran to meet him, and brought him into the house. Then he realized that his elder son was still out in the yard, and the father went out into the yard to be with his elder son. Had you ever realized that, according to the story, the father never returns to the house? That is the way Jesus told it, and that is powerful.

At one time, Jesus said that a physician goes where there is a need. The younger brother needed his father, and his father was there. His father brought him home and gave him a party. But the elder son was out in the yard. Now *he* needed his father—and his father went to him. The story never tells you that the father went back into the house. You can assume that he stayed out in the yard as long as he needed to; he stayed there as long as the elder son did.

That father is God. Jesus is not talking about a human father, he is talking about God. So, you are ripped off, you are cheated. You are never going to get what you deserve. Everybody goes through this at one time or another. Let religion help you. I'm not suggesting that you pray for God to punish other people or for favoritism. Instead, it's a matter of allowing religion to be real to us. What happens, I think, is that we become aware of God when we become aware of our need. However, we are so conditioned to thinking of God as strength and power that we become unaware of finding God in our weaknesses.

It is also vital to remember that our attitude is significant. How are we going to respond when we do not get what we deserve? We cannot control what other people do, but our reaction is so important.

I was talking with my mother over the phone recently when she mentioned that she had been visiting with a friend whom she has known for thirty-five years. She said, "Son, I've never seen this woman happy. She has always been worried in all the years I've known her. She frets all the time."

Mother mentioned this to her friend in their conversation. "I've never seen you when you weren't worried," she said.

Her friend said, "I understand that, Marguerite, but I've never seen you worried. Don't you worry?"

My mother replied, "No, I've never had a problem." Of course, she has had many problems.

Then my mother said to me, "Son, I told her, 'I've never had a problem, but I'm going to worry if I ever do have one. And the first thing I'm going to do is come and tell you about it.' You know, at my age," she added with a kind of chuckle, "I may never have a problem. Wouldn't it be something if I never got to worry?"

What kind of an attitude do you and I have? Life is hard on every one of us. We all have difficulties; we don't get what we want. How are we going to respond? One of the characteristics that we love so much about Jesus is the way he reacted to his problems. Did Jesus ever get what he deserved, for a single day in his life? Did anyone ever really understand him? Did anyone ever follow him, totally? Probably not.

Let's look at ourselves. We have been outside our home, in the yard, long enough, haven't we? Some of us have been out in the yard for a long, long time. But there is a party going on and it is in *our* house. Isn't it time for us to get up, come inside, and join the family?

3

Cain and Abel

Scripture: Genesis 4:1-16

The stories in the Old Testament are not only fascinating, they are also timeless. Some works can be contemporary and transitory because they do not contain a worthy principle. And some works can belong to the past and yet have a profound relationship to our lives today because they deal with truth. One of the reasons Shakespeare's work is so meaningful is that he deals with human emotions, which are the same today as in his time. We are intrigued by both his literary excellence and his psychological insights. On a more profound basis, the Bible grapples with the idea of who God is and what God requires of us. It asks, Who is my brother, my sister? How should I treat people? Who am I?

In the Bible these themes are introduced to us by a family that is representative of all families. The story of Adam and Eve is not an account written by someone who observed them; it is written from a different perspective. It is an effort to convey that in the beginning God made everything that was made, including the family. But the first man and woman, Adam and Eve, overreached their mark; they wanted to make their own rules. That got them into trouble. They were evicted from the Garden and could not return. In other words, they grew up. This was their curse, but also their blessing!

Columbus discovered a new world because he sailed in uncharted areas. Progress would have been stifled if his mind had been fixed on the known. To make progress, we must recognize what is already known, to some degree, and then launch out in an attempt to determine what should be or might be. After we do that it is not possible to go back to what we were before.

When we are twenty, we cannot be thirteen, though we may want to act like it at times. When we are forty, we cannot be twenty. That's the way it is; we cannot go back. It doesn't work very well if we try. You cannot put your hand into the same river more than once. You can take your hand out and put it back, but the river has changed. Even if it is dammed and not flowing, the molecules are constantly in flux.

Out of the Garden, "Adam knew Eve," which means they came together sexually. Eve gave birth to a child, Cain. Later she bore another child, Abel. Here, then, is the family unit, father, mother, and two sons. We tend to think that at this time there were only four people on the face of the earth, although we know this is not true because Cain later marries a woman in another part of the country. The story does not necessarily convey historic facts, but an idea that is true. We don't know from where Cain's wife came—we don't have to know. But other people were alive. The point of these early stories is that God made people, and it wasn't easy for them to get along with each other. They had a difficult time trying to find out who God is, who they were, and what their relationship was to other people.

Nonetheless, here we have the father, mother, and two sons, Cain and Abel. One day Cain and Abel decided they should make an offering to God. Cain was the farmer; he grew the crops. Abel was the keeper of the flocks. Each brought an offering to God to be burned on an altar, which was the way sacrifices were made in that day and time. The people didn't know that God didn't require this sacrifice. God didn't want a burnt offering then any more than he wants one now.

There is a great statement in the book of Micah: "What does the Lord require of you but to do justice, and to love kindness, and to walk humbly with your God?" But the people were not aware of that then, nor are we very often aware of it now. Out of their guilt and frustration, they made offerings to God.

Cain began to think that God was more pleased with Abel's sacrifice than with his. There are no reasons given for his feeling this way. However, we can guess—Cain may have felt guilty, perhaps because he was careless about his offering; he may not have brought the best he had, and Abel probably brought the finest animal in his flock. Cain's reaction isn't unusual. We are jealous of someone who beats us, especially when we didn't really try, when we cut corners.

It wasn't God speaking to Cain, saying, "I don't like what you did." Cain was dealing with himself, thinking, "I'm kind of a heel, bringing an offering when I didn't mean it. This is only a pretense; I'm not actually getting involved. Abel did a better job." So, from his own understanding, however narrow it was, he decided that Abel's sacrifice was more pleasing to God and he wondered what he was going to do.

One can only tolerate pain for so long. Then one must act. You know what Cain did—rather than dealing with his guilt maturely, by admitting that he felt like a fool, rather than admitting he had been remiss, Cain denied his guilt to himself. Therefore, he had only one other viable choice—which was to dispose of the one who was causing the problem. He would rid himself of the one who brought his guilt to mind whenever he saw him; he would rid himself of his brother.

He had the opportunity to do this one day. Out in the fields Cain killed Abel. Then God began to speak to him, though not necessarily in an audible way. God probably spoke to him the same way God speaks to us. He speaks through our consciences, our minds, our psyches, our beings, wherever we live, from deep within us. The Lord spoke to Cain and asked, "What have you done?"

Cain knew what he had done, but he was still trying to argue with himself. So he countered with a question, "What do you mean, Lord?"

God said, "The blood of your brother cries to me out of the ground. Where is your brother?"

"Am I my brother's keeper?" was Cain's response.

According to the story, God punishes Cain in this way: "As long as you live you will have to wander over the face of the earth. I will take the land from you; you will never be able to till it any more. You will not be a farmer, you will be a wanderer."

Cain objected to this punishment. "Lord, this is too much for me, I can't take it. You've taken my land from me; what can I do? People will try to find me and kill me."

"No," God said, "I will make it so they will not kill you. Whoever tries to kill you will be punished seven times over. But you will be a wanderer all of your life," implying that the people who follow him will also be wanderers.

The writers of this story had seen nomads, tribes who roamed throughout the area, with no settled homes. They thought these wanderers were being punished, and so they asked, "Why do some people have to wander? Why do they not have a home?" And since God took charge of everything, and anything that happened was the will of God, the answer was obvious—God did it. From an observation, a conclusion was drawn and this story was written to explain past events. Today when we read the story, we read it as if it were flowing forward. God didn't punish Cain and condemn him to a nomadic life. But, in reality, our own guilt can do that to us if we don't resolve it. Our guilt can create a kind of floating no-man's-land where we have no home even though we have a house, we enjoy no peace or security even though we have roots in the city. The biblical message is exciting because it deals with eternal principles that we can relate to and learn from.

At times, we are so very much like Cain. We justify our acts before we commit them. Cain made up his mind what he was going to do. Then a voice spoke to him saying, in effect, "Cain, don't do it. Watch your jealous nature; it is going to get you into trouble." But he didn't listen.

When we hurt ourselves and other people, we have probably run past roadblocks. We rationalize, however, which is why we can have war after war and call each one a righteous war. In most cases, wars have been fought under the guise of bringing peace. Hitler did that. People go to war talking of peace. Few people have gone to war just to have war. If our cause is right, we feel we are justified to declare war. That's Cain. There are four people on the earth, according to the story, and one fourth of them is going to attack another fourth.

At the end of World War I, the major powers gathered for the meeting at Versailles. Clemençeau of France was speaking of the demands made by the leaders of various countries. "No," the other leaders protested, "we want peace." And Mr. Clemençeau said, "If you are determined to ask for the lands that you want from the defeated countries, call it peace if you wish but you are laying the grounds for war." He was exactly right. Twenty-odd years later the world was plunged into a second World War.

You and I, if we are not careful, offer our excuses for something before we get into it. We rationalize, and the results can be disastrous. We can do this in our families, and that is exactly what Cain was doing. He made up his mind to excuse himself before he ever acted.

Cain excused himself so easily, perhaps because he was so very cognizant of his problems. When we spend so much time aware of our own problems, we become unaware of other people's problems. On the other hand, some of the most compassionate people in the world have developed their kindness because they knew they had problems. We see this in members of Alcoholics Anonymous. There are people in the healing professions—nurses, doctors, counselors— who have dedicated their lives to helping other people because they have had problems themselves. That's healthy; it's marvelous. But, at some point, if we are overly concerned about our problems, we become oblivious to the fact that other people have problems.

If you have been spending the majority of your time thinking about your problems and you are unaware that anyone else is suffering, you ought to check on yourself, because you are slipping. There may have been people who have tried to tell you this. You have read the newspapers, you live with other people, you have friends and neighbors; all kinds of things are going on in their lives. If I live for an entire week and never think of the agony that is going on in someone else's life, it is not that my problem is so enormous, it is that I have gotten it out of focus. That will make us sick. If we let our problems possess our minds, dominate us, we will feel so sorry for ourselves that we will be more concerned about a pimple on our faces than about a cancer in someone else's life. This is true for every last one of us.

About fifteen years ago, my wife and I had the mumps at the same time. That makes for a lot of togetherness, although I can think of better ways of bringing closeness about. But there we were, both of us incapacitated for days.

One day a man phoned the parsonage for help. He was going through town, he said, and needed some assistance because he didn't have any money. My wife apologized, and told him there was no way we could get to him to help him because we were both in bed with the mumps. He said, "That's just the way it is; I called you to give you my problem and you ups and gives me yours."

Sometimes we feel that this is how it is in life—who's going to listen to our problems? We can all have such episodes—they are normal and natural. But, if week after week we become so involved in our own problems that we are unaware of what is going on in other people's lives and almost assume they don't have any problems, then we need to take ourselves off our hands for awhile. We need to take a vacation from ourselves and listen to someone else. It isn't healthy or characteristic of a balanced life to be overly concerned with oneself. Cain allowed his problems to get out of focus, so what was he going to do? He would rid himself of his brother, Abel.

Most of us have been taught that disagreements are to be avoided. However, I'd like to suggest that we *ought* to have disagreements, but conduct them rationally rather than emotionally. Sometimes we need to have real discussions in our families about how things really are. We can't always be Pollyannas, saying everything's all right. Jesus faced issues, and faced them squarely. When he realized that he had to take a stand regardless, he overturned the tables in the Temple and stood there in full view of the crowds.

There is a time when we have to do that in our families, but it should be done with reason and not just emotion. We are so inclined to hurt people with words. We forget the principles we are dealing with and instead go to work on a person. We can be so cutting, so damaging. And then away from the situation, we feel guilty and realize we didn't mean what we said. There is a time when a disagreement is helpful.

Cain had a problem with Abel; he was jealous. Why didn't he say so? Why didn't he deal with his jealousy and say, "Look, you outdid me, but maybe I can learn a lesson from this. I didn't want to offer the best I had, I didn't want to burn it. But I want to be forgiven by God; I want to be religious. I want to be healthy, whatever that means"?

If we do not deal with what is bothering us in an honest and open way, the problem will come back to haunt us. There is no way to get around it. If we become jealous enough, and block our jealousy, then hostility and anger will build up and cause us to act in a way that, if we are not careful, will be more destructive than anything we would have ever chosen to do voluntarily.

When the Nicene council met in 325 A.D., their discussion centered on Athanasius, who proposed that Jesus was God, the same substance as God, and Arius, who said that Jesus was of like substance. Such a controversy may not seem to carry importance for us, but it is really quite significant. Most churches follow Athanasius' proposal, saying that Jesus was of the same substance as God. The discussion was heated, but it was conducted rationally.

Unfortunately, this has not always been true of the church. Hundreds of years later the church launched the Crusades. At that time the Turks possessed the Holy Land, what is again Israel today. The thought was, "It is a religious duty to take land from the Turks, because of the shrines and the holy places relating to the life of Jesus. God doesn't want those horrible people to desecrate them." It became honorable to join the Crusades, and to try to capture the land from the Turks. There was even a Children's Crusade. In this case, emotion held sway.

Today, if you and I aren't careful, by calling it love for America, we can justify whatever we want to do. From our own viewpoint, we can always make a war righteous. We can make it a holy war, upholding God while we trample on God's people somewhere else. And God weeps. A lot is expected of our nation because we have received a lot. We should exercise reason.

Our problem often arises because we want to do what is right. Families frequently have problems because someone is determined to be right. You can be right in one situation, but not another. And being right can blind you to the times that you are wrong.

Right is found by compromising, by adjusting, by being flexible, by compassion, by love, by justice. Jesus stood for what was right, but there was always that compassionate quality in his life, which was not true for Cain. We can see the inherent danger in a determination to be right and a refusal to recognize having done something wrong.

Years ago, when I was serving a small church, I was asked to serve on the town election committee and work at the voting booths after I had been in the community only a few months. I agreed, and it wasn't long before I noticed that when the blacks came in to vote, someone would stop them at the door and tell them they were glad that they had come to vote and they would vote for them. That was it. I'll admit it was a fast way of voting.

As soon as I saw this happening, however, I went to some friends of mine in the polling area and said, "You can't do that. You can't vote for these people."

"Preacher," one man said, "you don't understand. This is the way we have done it around here for years."

I persisted until, finally, they said I was right, and they began to let the blacks come in and vote. It was marvelous that I was there. I was so glad to be able to help the church and change the voting procedure of the county. But, when we got ready to count the votes at the end of the day, we could not find the ballot box. I do not know when they stole it. I didn't see them take it; it was just gone. They said they were shocked. Don't you know they were! Well, after awhile, they counted the ballots and their candidate had won, which was not surprising at all.

I left the election hall that night frustrated, irritated, and pious, thinking that we needed to have a lot of education in that little town. Later, I began to view the incident from other perspectives. I felt good about standing up for the right cause. And I *was* right. It was wrong not to let the blacks vote; it was silly and inexcusable. But I had never worked to get a job for any of the black people in that town. I didn't visit any of them when they were sick. I didn't know what was happening in their lives. I never helped any of them financially. Still I went back to that parsonage after the election feeling so righteous. I was right in that one instance, but it didn't need to stop there. My idea of being right just let me close myself up; I didn't have to do anything to get jobs for people while some men were taking whatever amount of money they had, which wasn't much, and employing others.

What really happened that day? Both views were wrong. That's the honest way to look at it. It is never a question of your being right and somebody else's being wrong; God cannot get through from that viewpoint. The appropriate response is, "God, we are both wrong, have mercy on us."

That's also where we solve our problems in our families. You can argue forever about how right you are. Perhaps both of you are right, in a sense, but insisting on that is going to push you farther apart. Let's stop trying to be right. The world doesn't need any more of that gimmickry. We don't need window dressing to be impressed with somebody's goodness. Let's just be honest. And then before we know it one of us will be reaching out to touch hands, to say "I'm sorry; I'm wrong. Maybe I have been right in some things, but I have been awfully wrong in a lot of others." Cain needed to *see* that.

We also need to recognize that we have not always told the truth. We don't have to do our dirty laundry in public, but we should stop trying to remake the world in our image; we should stop thinking in terms of giving a witness to the world by making prototypes of ourselves. The world doesn't need that. We should recognize our guilt.

One day in an almost casual conversation, a woman began to tell me repeatedly how much she loved her mother, how she idolized her mother. She said several times that her mother, to her way of thinking, was the finest person who had ever lived. I began to realize that this insistence was abnormal. Obviously it was right for her to love her mother, but this was an exaggeration and not healthy.

Finally, I said, "Something is driving you to say this; something is wrong with your approach." The woman became very irritated with me and disagreed with my statement. The next day, however, she came back to see me to tell me how she hated her mother and had despised her for years, but she had felt so guilty about it that she couldn't say it. And then she burst into tears. After awhile, she said, "I really love my mother."

Now she is healthy; she is well. Her mother had hurt her. Maybe her mother didn't mean to hurt her; perhaps her mother meant well. But, in the process of living with people, we get hurt at times, and the one to whom we are the closest can hurt us the most deeply. This woman needed freedom to admit she despised her mother. God can understand and accept that. The moment she admitted her true feelings and let them out, she was on the road to health.

Cain, however, did not allow himself to do that. He was jealous but couldn't recognize it; he was angry but he wouldn't admit it. What happened? He grew hostile and killed his brother, Abel.

When you are guilty, admit it; *say* it to yourself. You have not always kept your word; you have not always been what you wanted to be. Don't you know God knows that? To become a better Christian, do not pretend.

Learn just to be. You don't need to pretend any longer; just live with yourself as you are. That's what Cain needed in his relationship with his brother, Abel. That's what we need in our families. Unfortunately, we are almost led to believe that if we are converted enough, we won't have to cope with real problems any more. We will have thrown our guilt on the Lord—we will be able to walk away. We will have given our minds to God—he will make every decision for us. On the contrary, God gives our lives back to us. We are responsible under God. Cain needed to hear that too. The church needs to hear that. America needs to hear that. We will never find a panacea to solve every problem. If we did, the results would probably be disastrous.

When you give your life to God, God gives your life back to you. It's as though he says, "I gave you a complete kit, a do-it-yourself kit, and I'm going to work *with* you, but don't throw it back on me. Go on and accept your guilt; that's the cutting edge of life. I'm with you; I love you; I'm involved with you." This is like the father of the prodigal son running out and accepting his son as he is and saying, "Come home like you are." If we don't do that, live with ourselves, accept ourselves, we become our own enemy.

One day Cain and Abel were out in the field. Cain fell on his brother and killed him. The world has seen this so many times since, it is almost unbelievable. We call it history; one country against another, one tribe against another, one family against another, one individual against another, one person against himself or herself. There is another way.

"Lord, I want to ask *you* a question: Do you think I am my brother's keeper?" God doesn't give a direct answer, but there is an answer. "No, Cain, that's not really what I had in mind. Abel is your *brother*. As much as you are a person, he is a human being, too. You are not your brother's keeper, Cain, *you are your brother's brother.*"

4

*F*ather

Scripture: Luke 2:15-19

Even if we live alone, we are involved with people. Therefore, in a sense, we all have a family association. Many of us are supported by a family, loved by a family, hurt by a family. Our family experience doesn't simply prepare us for life, it is life itself. What takes place in this experience and our interpretation of it is of the utmost significance. It will forever make a difference in our lives.

Let us explore this idea by considering Joseph, in the New Testament. Its treatment of his life is interesting—Joseph is propelled on and off the biblical scene as quickly as possible. At times he is ignored. When the shepherds came to Bethlehem and spoke of what they had been told, the scripture reads, "But Mary kept all these things, pondering them in her heart." What about Joseph? Did Mary make plans by herself? No. Joseph was involved.

One popular way of reading his story is to say that if God is the father of Jesus in a biological sense, then Mary became pregnant by God and Joseph had nothing to do with her pregnancy. That is concise and direct. Mary, as a young girl, was frightened when she realized she was pregnant. What was she going to do? She went to visit a relative, Elizabeth, and told her about her condition. Can you imagine how easily you could be ostracized at that time in that culture? A woman could be stoned if she were caught in adultery. If you are pregnant and not married, it is quite obvious what you have been doing, isn't it? She was to marry Joseph, but he did not want to marry her when he found out she was pregnant. Then an angel appeared to Joseph, explaining things to him, and he decided he would marry her. That is the story.

Still, a problem exists however the story is explained. Joseph is important to the scene. Why? To appease gossip? Did God think, "I must get some man to come and be with her, so people will not ostracize her. We will use him, speak to him. He is a part of our plan"? Is that the way it worked? That's one way to read the story, of course.

But here is another way: Joseph is a young man you do not read about very often; there aren't many words written about him. He married Mary. He took her to Bethlehem for the tax registration. There was no place to stay when they arrived, but he found a stable, where the baby was born. That required some arrangements did it not? We can assume Joseph didn't have much money because he offered only two pigeons when Jesus was dedicated at the Temple. That was equivalent to two pennies. It was the smallest offering he could have made, unless he had offered only one pigeon. Being aware of this offering is like looking at Joseph's financial statement. It tells us he didn't have any money, because a good Hebrew would make an offering in keeping with his financial position when he had a child dedicated. This young man didn't have any money, but he was taking care of his wife and his son.

Joseph also had to face fear. The male babies, those two years old and younger, were being killed because King Herod was so threatened, so frightened by a child. Isn't it amazing what can scare us? When we are ill, when we are paranoid and our egos are inflated beyond all normal proportions, we become so sick that anything can pose a threat to us. A king was afraid of a mere baby! He reacted by ordering "Kill them!"

So Joseph took Mary and Jesus and went into Egypt. That was a long journey. From Bethlehem to Egypt is a lengthy trip even today, not just in terms of miles, but also in terms of all the journey's involvements. This is particularly true when you don't have much money. They sought safety in Egypt, where they stayed for quite some time—we do not know how long. Later, they came back to Nazareth, where Jesus grew up.

One day, when Jesus was about twelve years old, Joseph, Mary, and Jesus went to Jerusalem. It was important to go to the Holy City for Passover when you could. If you lived within a certain radius, it was almost mandatory that you go once a year; you certainly had to go during your lifetime. Devout Hebrews wanted to go at least once a year. And now Joseph, who was still a young man, took Mary and the boy Jesus to Jerusalem. How excited they must have been!

After the celebration they started home, Joseph thinking Jesus was with Mary, and Mary thinking he was with Joseph. That's understandable because the men and women did not travel together. They would separate to travel, as a protective measure, and then would meet at nightfall. Some men would lead a group of travelers, while other men followed behind. The women and children were kept in the middle in order to protect them. So when they camped at night, they realized Jesus was not there. They had to go back into Jerusalem, a day's journey, to look for him. It took another day before they found him in the Temple.

Notice this: Mary asked Jesus, "Why did you do this to us?" That's the way you would say it if you thought it was going to be written in the Bible. If you lost your son for two days and you thought you were going to be read about, you would say, "How could you possibly have done this to us?" But, if you didn't think anybody was going to read about it, you know what you would say. You'd go straight to the point. Take note of what Mary says: "*Your father* and I were concerned." And Jesus responded to the word *father* and said, "Did you not know that I must be about my father's business?"

That's about all we know of Joseph. The narrative gets him on stage and off as quickly as possible. Mary, God, and Jesus—that's it. In a sense, that's the holy family to some people. But let's not deceive ourselves; Joseph is important. In every last one of our lives, the greatest contributions we make may never be recognized. Our truly worthwhile gifts often are not known. That is the way life often is, but it doesn't matter. We all have that experience—men, women, and children.

When you see a footprint in the sand, you assume someone has been there. Here you can see the footprint of Joseph. It is not pronounced; it is very subtle, but it is there.

Have you ever thought that Jesus had experienced Joseph as his father before he had the idea that God was father? What would it have meant to Jesus if God had spoken to him, as a little baby, saying, "I'm your father"? As an infant Jesus didn't know anything about a father. His knowledge, his vocabulary, had to arise from experience. If you learn Spanish while you think English, you have to mentally translate the Spanish into English to know what the Spanish means. When you learn a language well, however, you learn to think in that language and this comes by experience. Some people who are bilingual think in two languages. They not only speak Spanish, but also they think in Spanish. Jesus spoke Aramaic. Suppose, however, God had used Aramaic and had spoken to Jesus, as a little baby, saying, "I'm your father." This would have meant nothing to him at that time. But the baby grew into a little boy and Joseph was there. Joseph taught him how to be a carpenter. As a matter of fact, that is the profession Jesus followed for most of his life. The impact that Joseph had on Jesus is obvious. What kind of a father was he? I think we can assume he was a good father.

Later, when Jesus began to teach about God, he had a revolutionary idea that, from my point of view, is one of the most important thoughts you can deal with. The world is torn asunder by religious fanatics. In the name of God, we don't need more religion. But we do need more awareness of human dignity, more love; we need the Beatitudes. Yet religion so often divides us. When Jesus went out to teach about God—an idea, a concept—he called God "Father." Think what that does. It puts the idea of God in an emotional context. Where did he get that understanding? Look at Jesus' experience: he had been with Joseph. Can anything in the world be more complimentary than that? I realize it was a masculine culture. He would not have had the audacity to call God "Mother" at the time, although Mary has been elevated by the church. God is sexless, in this sense. God, for us, is a masculine concept, but we do not think of God simply as a man, although we refer to God as "Father." We can only learn of concepts to which we have been exposed. Even our own fantasies must be related to such experience. We cannot start with the fantasy and work back. We must begin where we are and work forward.

Jesus spoke of God as a father. Where did he get the idea? Perhaps from many places, but he knew a man; he knew Joseph. When Jesus wanted to talk about God, he said, "Father." Across the years, the church has not dealt with that idea very much. We just get Joseph on and off the scene as quickly as possible.

When we hear the word *father,* we often think of masculinity. And when we hear the word *masculine,* each of us responds. Some think of the macho type. What Sylvester Stallone is doing to us! I think Jesus was masculine, but I believe masculinity is also at times tender. When you are strong enough to be tender, you are strong. So often we assume you are tender when you have lost and you have to be. We think strength is a

Sylvester Stallone beating the devil out of people. I don't believe that.

One day a woman caught in adultery was brought to Jesus. Have you ever noticed that the man was not caught? I'm sure this has had to cross your mind. Don't you think there was a man with her? But it would have been unthinkable to have said a man was caught in adultery. That wouldn't have been allowed. So a woman was caught in adultery and brought to Jesus. Jesus, however, knew better; Jesus saw people, not situations. He loved people. I don't think there has ever been anyone who was more concerned about morality and upholding it than Jesus Christ. However, because he was so concerned about morality and people, forgiveness followed naturally. As for us, morality is not really our concern; we are concerned about fear, control, and appearances. Therefore, we judge.

Jesus forgave the woman. I imagine he did so for many reasons, and I suppose he did it out of his own heart. But where did he learn to forgive? Here was a man, but also a man kind and tender. The scripture states explicitly that he experienced everything in his mind anyone else has experienced. He knew what it was to be hurt and to want; he knew what it was to have conflict; he knew what it was to be tempted. What significance would his words have if that were not true?

How could he forgive a woman? I don't know, but I would imagine the young man had heard another story and knew it well—there was a time when his mother was pregnant with him, and a marvelous man, whose name was Joseph, loved his mother and stood with her to marry her. There was no stoning of Mary; let the petty culture do all the gossiping it could. That man stood by his mother, and that man was his father.

God is like that. God is our father, Jesus said. So of course he is going to stand by the side of the woman who is in need. In the name of God, Jesus is not trying to say everything is right. But he is saying, "The more something is wrong, the more you must work to make it right." He stood by the side of the woman in need, just as Joseph had stood by Mary.

How horrible it is today that people are captured and held hostage. I know of nothing more vulgar than raw power, although there does come a time when one form of power is required to overthrow another form of it. I am well aware of that. In a hostage situation, I find myself on the side of what I call total right, wherefrom the attempt is made to rescue the hostages, hoping they come out of the ordeal safely. I know that in order to do this rescuers have to use persuasion, diplomacy, and maybe another form of power, perhaps force itself, to rescue the hostages. But is anything more vulgar, more distasteful, to us than the full flex of muscle when it is used to hurt, degrade, dehumanize, destroy, enslave? Masculinity, on the other hand, is strong but also fraught with tenderness.

Masculinity also involves integrity. Integrity is certainly not confined to one sex, nor is it confined to upholding the existing culture in which it finds itself. It involves dignity, and though our society has many good aspects, we should continually try to refacet it to make it better. One judges a culture by asking, What is it doing to people, by and large? Jesus repeatedly challenged society; he took on the established church; he was outspoken about his culture; he was also a part of it. That's understandable. But if you take the idea of father, the masculine trait at its best, with the integrity that ought to be there, it seems to me that it is primarily concerned about human dignity.

Not long ago, I was with several other men who did not know I was a minister. We were having what might be called a general conversation. An older man and I talked about various things, nothing of any real significance. After awhile, I was having a conversation with someone else, but I could still hear the older man across the room. In a very loud voice, he was telling someone about a young black woman he had seen who had given birth to a mulatto child. "I walked over to her," he said, "and asked, 'Woman, is that your child?' And she said, 'Yes, sir.' I said, 'He's white; he has white blood in him, hasn't he?' She said, 'Yes, sir.' Then I said, 'I want to tell you, woman, you are a disgrace to humanity!' "

The man he was talking to laughed and asked, "What did she say?"

"She didn't say anything," the older man replied, "she just kind of smiled."

There may have been a disgrace to humanity on that day in the place he was describing; but it was not the disgrace he had in mind. I know nothing at all about the birth of that baby. There are all kinds of questions it might raise in people's minds. But, in the name of everything worthwhile, where do you think morality rests? Do you think that bigot of a man was actually concerned about morality? How can you be concerned about morality when you are not concerned about people's feelings? If he really thought she was a disgrace, why did he not try to help her? He was so righteous and pious. And what I didn't like about him is what I find in myself!

What do you think Jesus did? Not what *would* he do, but what *did* he do? He is a little better than we are, isn't he? Don't you suppose he was as good as the man I heard speaking? Don't you imagine he liked morality just as much as that man? But Jesus said to the woman caught in adultery, "I don't condemn you. Don't hurt yourself any more." Why would he do this? I think he did it because he loved God and he loved people. And where did he learn to love God and people? In a family. He remembered, "There was a time before I was born when my father, Joseph, stood by my mother." Integrity is always concerned about human welfare.

What is important is that we care. That is our contribution. Joseph need not be written about many times in the Bible for us to learn what he was concerned about; he cared about Mary and Jesus. Caring is what makes a person important; not whether many people know he cares.

Jesus was very aware of human frailties; certainly he must have been aware of Joseph's limitations. Yet, when Jesus chose to talk about God, he chose to say, "God is my father." Where did he get this idea? To a great extent, he got it from Joseph.

Years ago, a young woman came to me for counseling. She was teaching school in a very poor area, and she was afraid. Two or three older boys had, in a sense, threatened her. Not overtly, but she was afraid they intended to harm her. As it turned out, her problem was rather unique. She told me her father was in financial work in a large city. Eventually, I realized she was implying that he was in the Mafia. After awhile, I asked her if that were so. "Yes," she said, "that's what I'm telling you." Her mother had died and her father lived alone. He was obviously a very influential person. "If my dad knew that I was worried, you know he would take care of this problem for me immediately. But I don't want that to happen. I want you to help me find a way to stay where I am and teach, because I like my job; I want to help those kids. They have problems galore."

"Answer this for me," I asked her. "Growing up in your family as you have, with wealth, protection, and all the things money can buy, whatever led you to go into this kind of almost social work? What drew you to that?"

She didn't know, she said, but that was where her heart was and her father was very proud of her. And then she added, "I love my father, but he always taught me, from the time I was a little girl, that in order to love him I didn't have to be like him. He said, 'Don't be like me.' "

That's pretty good teaching, isn't it? You can hardly beat that. It is a healthy emotional idea: "I love you. You know I've made mistakes. I want you to love me, but don't defend my wrongs and weaknesses."

Jesus knew Joseph. I imagine that Joseph had no idea at all that when Jesus started talking about God, he would call God "Father."

5

The Judgment of Love

Scripture: Micah 6:8

When we think of God, most of us see him coming to us in the form of Jesus in Bethlehem. We see the child being born and placed in a manger. That is a sweet, comfortable kind of story; it ought to be important to us. It is filled with nostalgia and sentiment but it is also permeated with love and realism. This story combines the mystical and the very earthy in a marvelous way. That birth, we say, is to show us God.

But paradoxically we also think that some day we must face an austere God who will judge us. I do believe that we are judged, but I also believe we are judged by the God who revealed himself through Christ in Bethlehem. God is not inconsistent, is he? The story of the birth in Bethlehem tells us about God; it is not simply about Jesus. The story tells us about God and how God acts. We learn that the God who shows himself in that baby in a Bethlehem manger is the God we meet every single second of our lives, whether we are conscious of it or not. And that is the God who judges us.

We tend, however, to neglect that concept of God. In the church I suppose we want to scare hell out of people in order to manipulate them—to put more money in the collection plate, for example. We can fill our sanctuaries because so many of us are guilt-ridden and have to hear the idea of an austere God preached. In America, we emphasize the notion of earning every good thing that comes to us; we stress working for what we get. There is nothing wrong with working for what we get, but we can never earn the truly great things that come to us.

Can we earn our salvation? Can we say, "O God, I'm good enough; I deserve it"? We know we can never be good enough, nor can we earn our salvation by the right profession of faith. We cannot claim that God has to accept us because we've confessed Jesus as Lord and Savior. That's not the way it is. Our salvation is a gift. We do have to be humble to get it, but we don't deserve it, we don't earn it, and we never will. Furthermore, our salvation comes to us in ways we do not anticipate.

While the world needed the kind of person who would come and right the world, a baby was born, a helpless baby. That is God saying to us, "I'm like this, I need you." But we want to say, "God, I don't like that. Let me live on my low level, but God, *you* come and right all the world's wrongs. *You* feed the hungry, employ the unemployed, bring justice where there is injustice." Instead God seems to be vulnerable; God seems to be in need; God comes as a baby.

How do we learn to love except by being given the opportunity? A muscle becomes strong when it is exercised; a mind grows keen when it is honed. We grow in love by learning to love the helpless child. Isn't that the way it happens?

We are well aware of the austere God, and that image frightens us. Of course, there are scriptures that corroborate this picture of God. They say, in effect, "You'll stand at the judgment with no place to hide. Everyone will know your sins; God will know your sins." You are embarrassed, you are undone. I don't know what could frighten you if that doesn't. These scriptures are tantamount to the Holocaust, and there you are. They describe the judgment that way, and the explanation is that God is responsible for it. You can find many statements echoing this concept in the Old and also in the New Testament. However, when these statements are made, whether in the Bible or elsewhere, they are usually made by someone who is angry.

Think of it from this standpoint: Moses was angry when he came down from the mountain and found that the people who were supposed to be God's followers were worshiping a golden calf. But Moses was not angry solely because the Israelites had turned their backs on Yahweh; he was irate because they were not listening to him—to Moses. Moses' ego was hurt; he was the leader. How would you feel? Moses was infuriated. And because he was so enraged, he took the Commandments, the tablets, ground them up, put them in a solution, and made his followers drink it. You may not have known that this is in the Bible. I did not tamper with the text, it is there. We can read it and say, "Oh, he did that because the people had turned their backs on God." But Moses did it because they were not following him, and he had a good religious excuse to vent his wrath. Moses did it for the same reason you spank your child after he has repeatedly disobeyed you—you are exasperated. When that occurs, you are not dealing with your child in order to help him, you are responding because you are provoked. Moses had an idea of God, but he did not understand God fully.

How does Jesus explain God when people turn their backs on God? "Pray for those that despise you and persecute you." If we ask, "Jesus, why don't you take something, grind it, and make them drink it?" Jesus replies, "Why don't you listen to what I teach? Why don't you watch the way I act? When I do as I do, I'm not trying to get you to boast about me, I'm trying to show you what God is like." Yet in spite of Jesus' teachings, our world is permeated with the idea of the severe God who terrifies us because he plans to judge us.

We will be judged, but we will be judged by the same God who revealed himself as a baby being born in Bethlehem, his cradle a manger.

Images are important to us. Therefore, we treat as truth whatever we think to be true, whether it is or is not. If we think someone is our enemy, he is as far as we are concerned. The truth may be that the person thinks a great deal of you and likes you very much. Yet we respond to whatever we think to be reality as if it were absolute certainty. Furthermore, though we do have ways of verifying our beliefs, proof can be distorted by our convictions.

The stock market is a good example of this idea because stock often responds in the way we think it should. If enough people think a particular stock is a good investment, it may actually increase in value because these people will buy it. On the other hand, if enough people think a stock is worth little, they probably will not buy it and will sell it if they own it, perhaps even at a loss.

Years ago I was familiar with an international company that was extremely successful and fiscally quite sound. Its products actually sold faster than they could be produced. Economically speaking, the company's record was excellent, but its stock was decreasing in value almost daily. For various reasons, people were not buying the stock and those who had bought it were trying to dispose of it.

I also knew of another business in the same city, an insurance company. I visited with the head of this company one day. He was somewhat of a braggart. He was keen in many instances, and clever, but he was also very deceptive. His building was lavish. I remember sitting in his office when he very candidly told me what he intended to do. He said, "I've come here because I've studied the laws of this state and I know how to make a fortune by selling stock. I've established this insurance company, but I don't plan to make money out of it. I don't care whether people buy insurance or not. I'm going to make money out of stock." And he did; he made a fortune.

Some time later I was once again in the same building with one of the insurance company's employees. We were walking down a hall when he said, "Barry, come here. I want to show you something." We walked into a large room that contained rows of desks with typewriters on them, but not one secretary. Earlier, stenographers had been sitting at those desks as window dressing, as an effort to impress people. When I was there, the company did not even have one insurance salesman on its payroll. The employee told me, "I didn't know it was like this. I wouldn't have joined this organization. I'm getting out." The interesting thing about it is that this company's stock was soaring and it was not even a real company, just a façade. But people thought it was a money-making concern and they wanted in on it. They were rapidly investing in a sham.

We, too, can be like that. Whatever we decide is true is reality for us and nothing will change our minds. And then we find excuses to justify our astounding intellectual conclusions. Images matter; hence, there is a time when we must unlearn one idea of God in order to see another idea of who God is. What is his nature? What is his judgment? I would imagine his judgment is the one thing we should not fear. "What does the Lord require of you but to do justice, to love mercy and walk humbly with God?" God's love comes to judge us in a way that is in keeping with the presence of God we find in Bethlehem. We are to be judged, but we need not be afraid, for look who does the judging—the father of Jesus Christ our Lord. And what does Jesus tell us about God? Think of what he taught; remember how he lived; consider his birth.

When we think of the judgment of love, we should remember that love may never win, but it is always right and it will never be destroyed. Nonetheless, you and I want a winner. That's why we want a god with muscle. Herod had muscle. What chance would a baby have against the battalions of Herod? But where is Herod now? The Herods of the world have the strength but they never *really* win.

Indeed, love may never win, but it is right and it will never be destroyed. Did love win 2000 years ago in Bethlehem? Not on your life! Joseph and Mary had to flee to Egypt. Herod won. Even so, when you have the truth, you don't need any proof. A lie needs proof. If a person lies to someone, that person must gather all the proof possible in order to substantiate the lie, which is why many lies look so reasonable. On the other hand, honest people cannot generally tell anyone for sure, for example, where they were four weeks ago tonight because they weren't planning to have to tell anybody, they just were. But if you were doing something that embarrassed you at that time, you can probably offer a detailed excuse accompanied by an in-depth description of some place else that you happened to be.

When we read about Jesus being born in Bethlehem and then fleeing to Egypt, we realize Joseph and Mary took him there to save his life. Then some thirty-three years later, right before the cross, Jesus stood by Pilate's side. Barabbas was on Pilate's other side, and Pilate asked the crowd, "Whom will ye that I release unto you?" We know the response of the crowd: "Release Barabbas."

Then Pilate asked, "What would you have me do with Jesus, called the Christ?" The crowd said, "Crucify him."

We have assumed that if that crowd could have been sensitive enough to make the right decision, they would have said, "Give us Jesus and crucify Barabbas," and Jesus could have gone free. That's what we say we would have said if we had been there. But what would Jesus have done? Where would he have gone? I don't think he would have left. He would not have taken his freedom at that expense; if somebody must go to the cross, it would be him. "Crucify Barabbas," we can say, "he deserved it"; but what did Jesus say? "Inasmuch as you do it to the least of these, you do it unto me." Wherever there is pain, that's where God is, that's where Christ is. Love does not have to be set free.

How did we ever develop the mistaken idea that we were called to be Christians in order to become winners? Doesn't the world have a surfeit of winners? It has never had enough people who love. That's God's judgment on our world. We don't want God to judge us with love because we want to be hostile and to hate; therefore, we must have a god who hates his enemies, too. This is not Christianity, no matter how it is presented. Love is right; it never has to win because it will never be destroyed.

Now, it seems to me that one of the reasons this judgment of love comes is to show us our selfishness. How else will we be aware of this shortcoming? If I am not cognizant of my selfishness, I can walk all over your feelings and not even know it. Aren't we all like that? Yet love can come, and then I realize how small I probably am. When Jesus said, "Love your God with all your heart, mind, soul and strength and love your neighbor as you love yourself," we assumed that this was a commandment. Actually, it was a factual statement; factual because that is the only way we can love God and love our neighbor. That is the hell of it, and also the heaven of it.

You see, we look at other people in precisely the same way we look at ourselves. If I do not care for myself, there is no way I can care for you. I may be nice to you in order to get you to do what I want, but I don't really care for you. And, if I despise myself, I'll see a god of wrath. In that case, I must have a god who will burn people up, and rejoice because those people didn't know his name. Jesus is saying, in effect, "Tell me how you look at God, and I'll tell you how you look at yourself. Tell me how you look at people, and I'll tell you how you look at yourself."

You will do well if you will let the grace of God through Christ come to you and accept you as you are. So tell me how you look at God and people, and I will tell you how you look at yourself. You will love God and you will love people if that is exactly the way you see yourself—as loved. Love does that for us, not criticism, not harsh judgment, not the kind of judgment that sits on the outside and decrees simply, "You're bad or good, right or wrong." Love is not a teacher who comes merely to grade a paper; love stands by to help us work out the problem.

Love comes and we are no longer the same. I cannot lie to myself continuously after love comes. I no longer want my way all the time. Love makes a difference. It is both the most marvelous thing in the world and the most painful thing in the world. When we love, we join the human race. We were spending our time living for ourselves, and now we find happiness in living for people. They are no longer our enemies, our competitors. We can rejoice when they rejoice, and we will weep when they weep. This is not voluntary behavior, it is involuntary because we have fallen in love with love. That's why I think the world needs the gospel of Christ—his judgment of love comes to help us see our selfishness.

Quite frankly, I think selfishness may be the basic element behind all our sin; perhaps every sin we commit stems from selfishness. If this is true, how will we ever break the cycle? The only answer I can give is the love of God through Christ, alive in our hearts.

Finally, let us never forget that we do not have to be afraid of God. We need not fear the God who revealed himself in Bethlehem as a baby born and placed in a manger. The wise men and shepherds came; they stood by and watched. Apparently, they wanted to pick him up and cuddle him the way we want to love a baby. This is God's love in the world, God's judgment on the world. What does God think of you? Read the story of the birth in Bethlehem. That is what he thinks.

God comes to us. We need not fear him. God sent himself into the world in the form of Jesus Christ. We don't have to be afraid of God because we are not afraid of Jesus and Jesus shows us God. The story of

Jesus' birth tells us about the judgment of God on the world; the judgment is a story of love.

Many years ago, when I was very young, my sister and I decided we wanted to give Santa Claus something, so one Christmas Eve we placed a pair of socks and a soft drink beneath our Christmas tree. Several days later, my sister realized that our father was wearing Santa Claus' socks! That was a shock. My sister began to cry and said to my mother, "Look, Daddy is wearing Santa Claus' socks!" I said, "I'll bet he drank that Coke, too." And I imagine he did. Now I realize that what occurred was better than I thought it would be because my sister and I, having originally intended to give a gift to some unknown image, in the end realized we were dealing with our own father—one and the same person.

Isn't that how it is? When we realize this truth, we can say, "God, I thought you were going to judge us; I thought that's the way it was going to be. But what you have done is love us, and I guess, God, that's the way we're judged." If God comes and judges us with harshness, we can excuse ourselves because we tried. We just weren't smart enough or strong enough. But when God judges us with love, something happens to us. Our world needs that.

The world needed it two thousand years ago because the earth was so dark. A star was shining and not many people saw it. However we explain the star, we can sometimes hear the marvelous, mystical, mythical sounds of the angels. They don't even have to be there, do they? And at times, we can love just by sitting in a room and feeling close to people. The people don't have to be with us. We must however do more than merely live in a world of fantasy—we must also express our love.

If God loves you through Christ, isn't it inexcusable for you not to love yourself? And when you love yourself, listen to the man who is the Master, who speaks to you very clearly: "Now, loving yourself, by the grace of God you're going to love people as you love yourself. And you're going to love God like that because you realize that's the kind of God he is."

A baby was born and placed in a manger . . . that is the story. It is also the judgment of God upon his world, and it is better than we thought it was ever going to be.

6

*U*nhappiness

Scripture: 1 Kings 19:1-4

We often say we don't want to be carried away by our emotions. At other times we are concerned that we are victims of our emotions. Most of us have some difficulty knowing precisely what we feel at a given point; and so did Elijah. Let us look at his story.

In order to interpret this we need to realize that at that time, in the Jewish mind, God controlled everything that happened. If a drought came, God had caused it. If war came, God caused it. If locusts came, God caused that. If something good happened, that was also due to God. Whatever happened was the will of God. The people of that time were wrong however; they were mistaken in their understanding of God.

Surely we understand that God does not control everything. He would be a little God if he did. Think of the teaching profession: a little teacher is one who wants to control the whole class; a great teacher is one who wants to deal with an idea. Or think of a home: a small parent wants to be sure that he or she is in constant control of everything; a greater parent wants the children to develop their full potential. There is all the difference in the world between the two. Little people want to control; more mature people want to enable.

God was seen as a little God in Elijah's day, because the people saw themselves as threatened. When their land was parched and barren, God was responsible. That's what they believed and that's what Elijah preached. I do not know how to say it more clearly: Elijah was mistaken. But, he lived long before the time of Jesus and he didn't know better. However, we live long after the time of Jesus and we don't know much better either. The ridiculous things we blame on God today are absolutely inexcusable.

We do so many of the things we do because we want to, and then we may blame our actions on God. We may say, "The Lord made me do it," or the devil or whatever else. But, by and large, the reason the world is in such a hellish mess is that we make our own choices. The condition of the world is not the will of God, yet God's presence is in the world and his presence is our hope.

There was a drought in Israel in Elijah's day. Elijah believed that God was causing it because the people had sinned. Then he decided the drought occurred because they were worshiping Baal and, if they would get rid of Baal worship, of Baal's prophets, then Jehovah would reward them with rain. So he set up a contest. Elijah said to Ahab, "Get your prophets of Baal together and I will come. We will see which one wins." The prophets of Baal gathered and built an altar. They began to march around it, praying that it would be consumed by fire. Elijah loved this; he is almost childlike at this point. He became so excited that he began to taunt them, saying, "Why don't you shout louder? Maybe your god is asleep or maybe he is taking a journey."

Sometimes ridicule is the cruelest of treatments. We pretend we are complimenting someone and we do it with a jeer; we smile with a sneer. Elijah was enjoying this.

Yet we are not really in a position to criticize Elijah because that is the way we operate, too. Elijah was like a cheerleader, he couldn't wait to win. He was saying, "The winner shows the power of God, and that is what the world wants." The world says, "Give us a God that can zap it to them before they zap it to us!" This is not the Christian idea of God, but Elijah lived before Jesus. We live after Jesus however and yet the theological difference between Elijah and us is often microscopic.

To continue with the story, there was no fire, and the altar to Baal was not consumed. Elijah then built his altar to Jehovah, and his followers even saturated the altar with water to make it difficult to burn. Then Elijah said, "If Baal be God, worship him; but if Jehovah be God, worship him." He called upon God to consume his altar with fire: "O God, it will show you are God." And, according to the story, lightning struck the altar and burned it. As it is written in the book of 1 Kings, this incineration showed the power of God, according to Elijah, and Elijah was now the winner.

And, since he had won, he was going to thoroughly enjoy his victory; he was going to revel in it. He had the prophets of Baal killed. He said he was following God, following Jehovah, but turn this over in your mind: what right did he have to speak that way? We've made God too little for too long. Elijah killed the prophets of Baal. He didn't know that God didn't want that. How do we know? Because Jesus didn't want it. Jesus didn't hate the people who hated him. Slap him, he doesn't slap back; spit on him, he doesn't spit back; crucify Jesus, and he prays for you—that's God! Don't you think God was like that when Elijah was alive? But Elijah didn't know it, and we do not understand this concept of God very well either.

After that, Elijah turned to a man and said, "Walk over to the edge of the mountain, look out into the distance, and you will see a cloud." There was no cloud. "Look again!" Elijah ordered. The man looked several times and then he said, "Now I see a cloud, a dark cloud. It's in the shape of a hand." Then Elijah said, "It's going to rain," and it did. Now Elijah was convinced that God had given them rain because they had killed the prophets of Baal.

Elijah thought Jezebel, the queen, would be happy about what had happened. When Ahab started back home in his chariot, Elijah was so elated that he ran ahead of the chariot. Upon arriving home, however, Elijah was shocked to discover that Jezebel was not delighted he had killed the prophets of Baal. I don't know why he was so surprised. He had killed all of her prophets; I wouldn't have expected the queen to be pleased. When Jezebel heard what he had done, she said, "Send word to Elijah and tell him that if I don't get him tomorrow, about this time, I hope the gods do to me the same as he did to my prophets or even worse." You know what Jezebel meant. She was saying, "Elijah, I'm going to kill you." So Elijah became unhappy, and I'd say he chose a good time.

Now, Elijah had to deal with reality, not with theology. He had to try to save his own hide; and in that, he is very much like we are. He ran. I don't blame him. Jezebel had a way of doing what she said. Elijah left his servants and went a day's journey into the wilderness. There, he sat down under a broom tree, a juniper tree. He was totally depressed. He said, "O God, take away my life. I don't want to live; I am no better than my fathers were." Then he made this statement and reiterated it: "I, only I, am left." That betrays a pretty large ego. Elijah was convinced that he was the only good person in all the land.

If you want to be miserable, think of yourself in the same way. Elijah was saying, "O God, you have to depend on me, I'm the only one left and you might as well kill me." Well if that's all God has to depend on, he is in pretty bad shape. There were however many other prophets just as good as Elijah. As a matter of fact, the governor of Ahab's palace, Obadiah, had kept a hundred prophets in a cave secretly. He had taken food and water to them. Elijah knew that, but he was filled with self-pity, saying, "God, I am the only honest one left. There is no truth in anyone else. I am the only true prophet, God. I have tried and failed, so you might as well take my life."

All of us become depressed periodically. If we are healthy, we don't live on any one level all the time. We will be elated one day and unhappy another. But those times should not come too close together. If the highs and lows come very close together, say in the course of a few hours, unless of course you are going through an unusual experience, the chances are that you are not very well. But, in the course of a week or two, most of us will experience both some optimism and hope, and some disappointment, because we are dealing with reality. We experience a blend of feelings.

I hope that you are usually optimistic and full of hope, but there are times when a healthy person is unhappy. It is perfectly normal. We are not to live on just one level, however, and if most of your life is being lived in sadness, I think you ought to see a doctor. The cause may be physical, or it may be psychological, or spiritual. Unfortunately, the church tends to see the spiritual approach as the answer to every problem, which is ridiculous. When you have a broken arm you have a physical, not a spiritual, injury. We must not overly spiritualize something; just go and get it treated. Sometimes we are depressed because we are physically ill; it's that simple.

Several things can make us unhappy periodically. One of them is the pressures that are endemic to contemporary life. Take, for instance, instant reporting. Something happens in one part of the world and we know it almost immediately. That was not the case even one hundred years ago. At that time, without modern methods of communication, we were protected because we were unaware of so much that occurred. Today, during an election, we can hear the projected results even before we vote. Instant reporting has both made our world smaller and exposed us to an overabundance of news that is sometimes more than we can handle. This is not meant as a criticism of our news media or of our scientific developments, but merely to show that we now sometimes receive more than we can handle.

We live in a day of change, in which practically every area of life requires us to make adjustments. We want to do better, yet we almost resent that desire. At times the very situation in which we live is almost a threat to us. So, it seems to me, we absorb a sense of dejection.

I also think we sometimes grow heavy-hearted because we feel we have been cheated. Maybe we love someone and that person doesn't love us any longer. Or, the person we love dies. It is strange but true that losing someone in death often makes us resent them because we feel, to some degree, the person is to blame for dying and leaving us. We know that this is not right, but we do feel deserted; we wanted to keep the person with us. In the midst of this kind of pain and sadness, we need to recognize that we are also angry. We want to rail at someone, but we don't know whom to blame.

So there are times when we are hurt, feel cheated and deprived, and therefore sad. That's understandable.

At other times we may be unhappy because we have a poor opinion of ourselves. Recently I read about a young man who was traveling across the country by wagon train. A substantial number of the young people in the group with him had been in reform school. One seventeen-year-old boy who had been in reform school was asked what he thought about their trek by covered wagon. He said, "In all of my life, I do not think I have ever done one decent thing, and I love doing this."

Can't you relate to that? I'm not saying that when people break into homes or buildings we ought to excuse their actions and let them go; not at all. We need laws; we need to protect society. But I can understand how someone who has been depressed for a long time can become disgusted and take his feelings out on society. It's an unwell way of asking for help.

Teenagers particularly suffer periods of unhappiness. They are tested for everything in the world, and in this barrage of examinations, we have almost reached the point where we are saying to them, in effect, "We want the achievers, the winners, in our colleges and universities. We only want the salutatorians or the valedictorians," which is ridiculous! The world probably moves farther, longer, on the backs of ordinary people than it ever does on the rare geniuses. Whether that is true or not, we belong to a church that came into existence because a man from Nazareth thought it was true. He started something for the dropouts. Verify this: Jesus is not against underachievers—he is for them.

On the other hand, regardless of how much some of us win, we sometimes also fail. Let's not kid ourselves! We don't win at everything. And winning often requires bluffs, or even lies. If God only likes us when we win, God doesn't like us! If we only like people when they can produce, we don't really care about them. A mother cooks, cleans the house, and tends to all kinds of details. When she is ill and cannot perform, what is her value? She is worth more than any single deed she ever did in her life. I doubt if we understand that, but we follow one who did.

So there are times when we are unhappy because of pressure, because we feel cheated, or because we just have a poor opinion of ourselves. And sometimes our situations and our feelings are almost too much for us.

When we are depressed, as all of us are at one time or another, it is a good idea to make some changes in our lives. We can do that. If you have been working hard, take some time off. If you haven't been working, get busy. If you have been spending a lot of time with your family, do something else for awhile. If you haven't been with them much, spend more time with them. Make a change, as long as the change itself is not destructive.

What affects us adversely is the feeling that we must continue our routine forever. Even success affects us this way. Nothing can create more despondency than thinking we must hit a home run again tomorrow! If you are despondent, make some kind of a change in your life. Use your imagination; don't be a victim of life. Look at your life in a different way; don't see it fixed permanently as it is. A vision of an interminably unchanging situation can kill us psychologically, mentally, and spiritually.

In addition, we need to select our moods. We can do that, too. Don't get up in the morning feeling you are gripped by a mood and you must live in it. You can choose how you are going to feel. The people who live successfully, by and large, do that.

Jesus had more disappointments in his life than anyone else I know of. But reading the Gospels, I don't feel as though I am reading about a failure, because he had an approach to life. We too can select the mood we are going to live in. When we are unhappy, it is justifiable to let ourselves feel it for awhile, or if we are hurt to let ourselves be sad for awhile. We should recognize our feelings and say to ourselves, "I'm hurt and I'm just going to be like this for awhile. But later, I'm going to come out of this." Go on and admit your hurt and sadness, but don't you dare live in that frame of mind forever, because that is inexcusable. You and your life deserve more than that.

Most importantly, realize that God is with you. God does not wait until you get better. God does not wait until you are converted. As a matter of fact, we are never completely converted, just as we are never totally educated. Do we ever have all knowledge and wisdom? God is with us wherever we are. He is there when we least expect it and when we least deserve it. Certainly, God is always there. Tell yourself that. Whatever you are facing, whatever is frightening you right now, whether you are worried about your marriage or your job, a health report, the health of the one you love, whatever it might be, the same God who has been in this creative process all these eons is with you now, and you are with that God.

Let us think again of Elijah. Elijah is so depressed, sitting out under the broom tree. This is a great statement and it is written poetically: "There was a wind, but God was not in the wind; there was the earthquake, but God was not in the earthquake; there was the fire, but God was not in the fire; there was a still, small voice and God was in that."

I have never once heard from God in an audible way, nor do I want to. What language would he speak to me in—English with a Texas accent? I don't long to hear that. But I do know God. I would rather live by faith—in the awareness of where I am and in the awe of where I would like to be. I do not need another proof.

Let us extend our knowledge, expand our minds, and let us grow as much as we can. We know what it is to hear from God; we sense it. It is a voice that is not heard; a presence that is felt; a knowledge that is experienced but not understood. We know the still, small voice that comes to us, that is always with us. And sometimes, strangely enough, we are more aware of it when we are unhappy.

All kinds of exciting things may go on, dramatic things, but God is not in those things for you. However, when you are alone and quiet, there is a still, small presence and that's God! That is what will see you through your sadness. You know that, don't you?

7

Using People

Scripture: Deuteronomy 7:1-11

During the time recorded in Deuteronomy 7, the Israelites were nomadic tribes. They wandered for a period of time, and finally settled in Egypt, largely because food was plentiful there. They were probably content to be in Egypt for awhile, where they felt some sense of security. However, over a period of time, they were enslaved and then, for obvious reasons, they decided they would be better off somewhere else.

During the enslavement of the Israelites, while the plagues were besieging Egypt, Moses would go to the Pharaoh, king of Egypt, and say, "Yahweh did this; you had better let us go!" Finally, the Egyptians' children died, and again Moses went to the Pharaoh and said, "See! Yahweh is torturing you. You had better free my people and let us go!" God was not doing those things, but Moses probably thought he was, and the Pharaoh was superstitious enough to believe his explanation.

Think about it. What kind of God would send plagues? You may argue, "But the Bible says God did it!"—and it does. But later, Jesus taught a different idea: "Bless those that curse you. . . . If someone slaps you on one side of your face, turn the other side. . . . If someone compels you to go with him one mile, go two." Are you called to be better, more moral than God?

Moses was doing as well as he could as he plodded along, blaming his own very personal prejudices on God. And we do that today. But why, after all this time, do we still insist on clinging to the idea that God controls us but masquerades that control as love?

At last, the Pharaoh agreed to let the Israelites go. And, as they tried to return to their own land, many of the Egyptians who followed them were drowned in the Red Sea. The Israelites decided God killed the Egyptians. They reasoned that God belonged to the Hebrews and the Hebrews belonged to God. Following their escape from Egypt, they wandered in the wilderness for many years. Moses made it clear that Yahweh would protect the Israelites as long as they were faithful to Yahweh, but when they turned their backs on him, he would punish them.

According to the book of Deuteronomy, the God of all life, the God of all creation, the Father of our Lord, Jesus Christ, is supposed to have made this covenant with the Hebrew people:

> I will lead you into a land of milk and honey, into the land of Canaan; and you will destroy the seven nations which are already there, even though they are all stronger than you. I selected you, not because of your great numbers, but because I

chose to love you and I will be merciful to you and will give you the land for your own. When you take the land, kill all of its inhabitants and tear down their altars. Don't intermarry with them, because if you do they will persuade your children to worship their gods, and I want you to worship me only. I want you to destroy them—every man, woman, and child—because you are a holy people and I am a holy God.

What was so holy about that? Nonetheless, the Hebrews moved into Canaan and conquered it after waging battle after battle. They claimed the land as their own, saying, "God gave it to us." If that is true, I hope the Hebrew at his best, as he tried to discover what God was like, would have dared to ask himself the probing question, "Where does the Canaanite sleep tonight?" I am not anti-Hebrew in saying that, I am anti-conventional Christian. I find very little difference between zealous fundamentalists, whether they are Jews or Christians, because they have turned Jesus into somebody he would never assent to if he were here physically. Jesus did not teach control, he taught relationships. He did not teach a God of might; he taught a God of love.

We want security. As a matter of fact, we want it so desperately that we will do almost anything for it. Perhaps due, in part, to our desire for security, many of us prefer to be in charge. And, if we cannot be in charge, the next best thing is to have someone in charge who is on our side. You and I feel threatened when we lose control, do we not?

We have a security system at our church that must be turned off before a certain door is opened. Otherwise, alarms sound and the security office, as well as the police, are alerted. The security men respond quickly, and there is a $35 charge for every unnecessary trip. Since this system has been installed, three persons have triggered the alarm—two janitors and myself. Some time ago I set off the alarm accidentally. Immediately realizing what I had done, I called the security office and identified myself to the operator. I asked her to intercept the security guard, because I didn't want to pay $35. She said, "The bell has already gone off, but I'll try to stop them if you can identify yourself. What is your code number?" I did not know the code number. She was insistent. Finally, I persuaded her to accept some other means of identification. She asked for my telephone number. I told her what it was and she agreed to try to stop the security men. I felt relieved until I realized that a burglar breaking into the church would have been able to read the number off the phone just as easily.

We do prefer to be in charge or, at least, have someone in charge who is on our side. There is probably nothing wrong with wanting some authority, but if this desire is a predominant factor in our lives, it can be destructive. We dislike being told that God is not in charge of everything, that God does not always resolve our problems as we would like, and that we are not always going to win. We object to the idea that anyone is free to disagree with us. In reading this text, we can think, "Don't tell me the Canaanites were valuable people! Do you really think they loved their families as much as the Hebrews or the Christians love theirs?'' This seems to be our attitude. We frequently take this stance because we feel we must belittle someone else in order to prove our authority. We want to control any situation that affects us, and often our exercise of control masquerades itself as love.

As long as the Hebrews were in Egypt they were protected to some degree. They had a place to sleep, food to eat, and they had some security. But, as soon as they recognized they were slaves, they began to look for a way out. You may allow yourself to be controlled in many areas, as long as you think the person exercising that control has your best interests at heart. But, when you think that person's main interest is only in his power over you, you are apt to rebel.

Sometime ago I read a book about a prominent American family, written by their longtime family chauffeur. He wrote about a time when the matriarch of the family came into the kitchen and found him drinking coffee as he visited with one of the cooks. He depicts the woman as being avaricious, although his judgment may be prejudiced. Whatever the case, according to his description, when the woman saw him drinking coffee, she asked, "Did you pay for the coffee?" He thought she was joking, and said that he had not. She then said in all seriousness, "It will cost you ten cents." Of course, he was embarrassed and probably angered by what he must have considered her pettiness. He had no change with him, so the cook gave him a dime. He put it in a little jar on the cabinet, and the woman walked out.

Surely having to pay a dime for a cup of coffee was not of great significance. What was important was that the woman used her demand to emphasize her position—and his. She wanted to be sure he knew who was boss. Wouldn't anyone resent that? We tend to shrink from pure control. We may be willing to endure many restraints, as long as the person exercising those restraints seems to have our best interest at heart. But we would like to avoid control for its own sake.

What can confuse us is that control often masquerades as love, saying, "I have done so much for you, will you not do what I ask?" God says to the Hebrew, "I have brought you out of Egypt; aren't you willing to do what I ask you to do?" Jesus says, "Follow me and you will find salvation; turn your back on me and you will go into darkness." But regardless of what other preachers, teachers, theologians, or any parochial biblical interpretations may say, either God loves everyone equally or God doesn't love anyone. Religion should help us discover that.

Either God is God, involved in the whole universe, larger than we could ever comprehend, or we have made him in our own image. Of course, we do not carve graven images to represent God, but we do something even more drastic—we promote false ideas about him. Regrettably, ideas are harder to change than any physical image. We have made God what we want him to be, and we have had God say, "This is my covenant with you, Israel: You Hebrew people are to enter the land and take it; and when you do, kill all the inhabitants—every man, woman, and child—lest they worship other gods besides me." Who would want to worship that kind of God?

Ethics and morality seem to be missing from such a concept of God, yet Jesus said, "Blessed are the meek . . . . Blessed are the merciful . . . . Blessed are the peacemakers." And, most unfortunately, our theological thinking has leaned more toward the covenant idea of God—a God who will destroy anyone who disagrees with him—than toward Jesus' teachings. Where were we when the Beatitudes were taught in Sunday school? Why don't we spend time reading them in our Bibles? Or, better yet, why don't we dare to allow our minds the most exciting experience imaginable—the experience of investigating and imagining what truth might be?

Perhaps the truth is that we don't want love; we want control. We fashion a God of control, one who is on our side, and we tell others, "He will destroy you if you disagree with us, because we are right." I don't believe that! Actually, we take control and masquerade it as love. You may do it with your family, with other individuals, or with your company. Most regrettably, we do it with God.

Now, despite the fact that we want to be in control, we may allow someone we really love to disagree with us and we will still care for that person. If I really care for you, I will continue to care for you despite our differences of opinion. If I mark you off because you disagree with me, that indicates I don't care very deeply for you. Instead, I like myself, my own ideas, and my own security. God will never mark anybody off because that person rebels against him. If he did, he would be less than God.

We know there is right and wrong, and there are rules we are expected to follow, but God doesn't get his feelings hurt and zap us to hell when we break his rules. We are hurt when we do what is wrong, simply because of what we have done. God doesn't have to punish us when we lie or cheat; our punishment is in lying and cheating. And if you really love someone, you will allow that person the freedom to disagree with you and love him just the same. That is a lesson most of us must learn in dealing with our families, and with other people as well. We simply cannot control everyone or everything.

One of the reasons for this is that people are more important than power, and they always have been. For a long time, we have been taught that religion is more important than people. The Old Testament prophets tackled that idea repeatedly, yet the idea persisted and we find it still, in the New Testament: "the most important thing is pure worship, religion, God." I don't believe that! You are sacred and important because God made you. People are more important than control or power. If you think about it, you will realize that this is true. In the long run, what times do you remember best? The times you have had your own way? To a degree. Your successes? Maybe, for awhile. But I believe you will agree that what really makes your life healthy is having a right relationship with other people, whether they feel the same about you or not, while hell is a broken relationship. Jesus taught that.

One final thought: we have seen that total authority is destructive; however, love does entail a certain control. If we really love someone, that person has some degree of control over us. This control however is voluntary, because if we love someone we will allow him or her a certain amount of control. When a parent loves a child, the parent is not entirely free. The parent continues to love the child, regardless of anything the child might do. Take the story of the prodigal son, for example. The father loved this son, and when he was yet a great way off, the father ran to meet him. The father wasn't concerned about what the neighbors might say or that his son had embarrassed him. The father had suffered because the son had hurt himself, yet these issues didn't matter. The father was controlled by the son, to a degree, because he loved the son.

God is like that. We picture God however as a big, powerful God who demands, "These are the rules you are supposed to follow. If you follow them, I will give you victory, and you will be fine. If you break them, I will punish you; and when others fail to follow these rules, I will send you out to destroy them."

Are you telling me your God commits murder? What about the commandment that says, "Thou shalt not kill"? When you really love someone, you will allow that person some control over you. It follows that if you love God, a God of compassion and love, a God of mercy, you will allow him, to some degree, to control your life. But that is because you love him and because you care, not because you fear him.

Jesus introduced us to a God of love. There is nothing new about this thesis. It is true that love involves some control, but this kind of control is not used for selfish gain. Love's goal is redemptive. It is like the good doctor dealing with a patient; the good teacher with a student; the good parent with a child. It is the good God dealing with his people.

I do not know what will happen in our world today, but I know from history that the Hebrews went into Canaan and drove the inhabitants out, saying, "God gave us this land and this is his covenant with us: We must kill all of the people because God gave us this land." I imagine someone did ask, "What about the Canaanites?"

Before we become involved in another war, I hope we will be sensitive and mature enough to ask ourselves, "What really matters in the long run—power or love? Is power where God is? Is he not in the midst of love?" Unless God is a God of love who loves even those who do not love him, and unless we become mature enough to care for people who do not care for us, I do not know where we can turn for hope.

8

Because of Eve

Scripture: Genesis 2:21-24

What is important in a story is the truth it contains, not whether it is factual. The passages in Genesis that describe the creation of Adam and Eve are not an account of actual events. Obviously, eons ago, no one took notes about God making Adam and Eve. Yet what a story it is; what truth it contains! And sometime, in the process of reading it, I hope we will begin to relate to it and think, "This is my story. It describes me."

The narrative in Genesis 2 is one of two in the book of Genesis dealing with the creation of woman. According to this story, Adam has been made by God and is lonesome; his life is not complete. So God puts him to sleep and, while he is sleeping, takes a rib from him and makes a woman. Then Adam says, "Her name will be woman because she was taken from man."

A description of how good the Garden of Eden was is included. We are told that the man and the woman could do anything they wanted, except they were not to eat of the fruit of a certain tree. However, that was the one thing they did do. They ate of the tree of knowledge of good and evil. This is considered a sin by classical religion. For so long the Judeo-Christian faith has said, "They sinned, so God condemned them."

Was what they did so bad? Would they have really been good if they had not done it? Are our minds not supposed to question, to grow? Of course they are. Adam and Eve were growing up and growing up always involves getting into trouble. The only alternative is to stay at home and never grow. We are born not only with the possibility of having a good life, but also with the necessity of having problems. We cannot grow without difficulty.

After they ate, the man and the woman began to be ashamed because they realized they were naked, and they made clothing for themselves out of leaves. Then God said, "This will be the punishment: The man, Adam, will have to work by the sweat of his brow. The woman will conceive and bear children. And all the Adams after him will have to work hard. And all the Eves after her will bear children and the pain of childbirth will be severe." As if that were not enough, they were evicted from the Garden, and they could not return. Nor can we. Did you ever try to return to a situation? There is no way; the situation has changed; you have changed.

Today, like Adam, men toil, work, and sweat. They cry, worry, and strain. We see it daily, worldwide. And, like Eve, so many women give birth to children and cry out in pain. They realize they have another mouth to feed. Some of the children are not wanted and this is sad. What is God doing during our times of sorrow? I guess he is *able* to ignore our pain. He is all-powerful, the Creator of everything; therefore, he can certainly do as he pleases. Do you think God ignores us and our problems? If he does, then why do we not create another God? We don't because the situation I have just described is not real. Men do have to work, and sometimes they cannot find work, and the work they do find is often hard. Many women also must work and bear and care for children. Sometimes there is rejoicing and sometimes there is sadness.

Yet through all of this, what is God doing? We know the answer to this question before we ask, because of a Man who grew up in Nazareth who made the answer clear. When you are hurt, God is hurt, and when you rejoice, God rejoices. Centuries ago people didn't know this, so they could react only to what they thought they knew. They thought they suffered because God was punishing them. I will stake my life on it—God never punishes anyone. Small-minded people have to punish; Hitlers and Napoleons have to punish. Great people don't punish; great people teach; they accept and love. "What about teaching people a lesson?" someone might ask. Well, how do you teach someone? With a whip? Punishment doesn't teach, it angers. God is more interested in the relationship he has with us than he is in punishing us. The world suffered then, and the world suffers now, but God is not responsible.

Supposedly, Eve was created from a rib of Adam. I used to hear preachers present this idea. They said that the rib came from Adam's left side, nearest his heart.

I have heard it said in a wedding service that the rib was closest to Adam's heart, and that this should make Eve feel very happy. If every time men fell in love they lost a rib, eventually the chests of some would be vacant. Eve wasn't made from a rib. Eve is Eve, and Adam is Adam, and we all came from God. One is not better than the other, even though that is the way the story was told because men were doing the telling. In their story, Eve could not appear to be better than Adam, so she must blame the snake for their problem. She could not possibly be a heroine and say, "God, I did it." From the men's point of view, that would ruin their story.

Who did cause the problem? Everybody, and nobody. We don't blame anyone, but we need somebody to take responsibility. I believe in universal salvation. I believe that when we die we are all going to God. Selfishness may make us want to believe we'll be the only ones close to God. Think about that. Does it diminish us to think that other people who are not exactly like us are going to be with God? The whole world goes to God, all of creation. That says nothing about us, and everything about God. We don't need the right belief in God so that we will go to heaven when we die. We need to let God take care of those decisions.

I see this story in Genesis telling us that we need an enlightened understanding of God, an idea of God as one who is compassionate, an idea that was taught by Jesus and the prophets at their best. I believe this world is the Garden of Eden, but *we* have made it a hell. We evict ourselves, and God is waiting for us, inviting us to come back, to re-establish the Garden. What more could we ask God to do other than what he has done? God does not punish us, we punish ourselves. Evidently, we are not as intelligent as we should be, because sometimes we deliberately do what is wrong. As a result, various consequences befall us. But what happens to us is not God acting to punish us for our sins. On the contrary, God works with us, trying to help us solve our problems.

One of the reasons some of us find this false concept of a God of retribution credible is that we feel we must have someone to blame. Periodically, each of us wants to blame someone.

One Sunday a problem occurred in the televising equipment just before our worship service was to be televised, although I was unaware of it at the time. Since it was time for us to go on the air, an old tape was substituted. As a matter of fact, it was five years old. In a few minutes, the television station corrected the difficulty and we were back on the air live, but, of course, our live service didn't jibe with the first few minutes of our old service. There were many discrepancies, and we received several phone calls. One caller mentioned that my hair was darker in the earlier part of the service. Five years does make a difference in some of us!

Who do you blame when difficulties like that arise? There is no one at fault, really you work hard and yet you fail; you attempt something and it doesn't work. You don't have to blame anyone if you have a problem in your marriage, in your business, or in your personal life. You may have worked diligently and prayed; yet you don't feel you are doing very well. Some people who love you and know you well may think you are doing fine, but at times, you still want to blame something, perhaps your childhood, your family situation, or your lack of ability. Assessing blame, however, does not solve the problem.

If Eve had been able to respond honestly to the question of who caused the probem, she might have said, "Lord, in a way we all did. And in another way no one did. We acted out of ignorance." Quite often, a problem is not caused by sin as much as it is caused by a lack of knowledge and understanding. We should accept responsibility and not blame someone else. Adam didn't have to blame Eve, and Eve didn't have to blame the snake. The snake already had an image problem. We don't have to blame anyone.

In addition to sometimes wanting to find a scapegoat, we share another trait with Adam and Eve: we like the excitement of adventure. I see the fall of Adam and Eve as a renaissance. What was their alternative? Should they have stayed in the Garden forever, simple and childlike? Is that what you want for your children? Children may be hurt when they reach out, but that is how they grow. We have developed fire, the wheel, the airplane, and have split the atom. We may misuse all of these advances, but that does not make their discovery sinful. The anticipation of adventure is part of our hope.

When a couple fall in love and marry, they have the potential of hurting each other very deeply, but it is worth the risk. What is the alternative, never to trust? The story of Adam and Eve is so often interpreted to mean that we will be in heaven if we stay in the Garden and do not use our minds. That's not true; that would be a hell. Should we live in this world and not explore it, live and not ask who we are and who other people are? The risk can be great; we can be hurt. We should understand that. There are sins we commit that can destroy us; we should be aware of that. Yet there is also within us that spark of life that causes us to want to inspect, to go beyond, to find out if the grass is greener on the other side.

We like adventure. We like surprise because the expected can be banal, but we don't like the pain of shock. At times we are threatened if we stand still; at other times we are threatened if we make a move. But there is a spark of life within us that longs for adventure. That may be the curse of our existence, but I say it is also the hope of our existence. For so long, people believed in the divine right of kings. For so long, we felt we had to have slavery. Ultimately, both of these beliefs were challenged. Ask questions and grow. People once thought that everything that happened was the will of God until someone said, "I don't believe that." Human life was considered cheap; God was everything and people were almost nothing. And then Jesus came, saying, "I know you have been taught to think in terms of an eye for an eye and a tooth for a tooth, but I say unto you that the greatest among you will be the servant; bless those who hurt you." He was presenting an old idea in a new way, the idea of being inside the Garden and choosing to go outside. That is questioning, growing, risking. Still we are frightened and we push Jesus' teachings aside. We ignore his words; we try to go back to being naïve, simple children. We anticipate heaven when we die, while we let our world go to hell. I think God calls us to come back inside the Garden to make our world an Eden once more.

Our hope is in not waiting until we die to live an ideal life; it is in living and thanking God we are alive in this world today. What if we were to solve the world hunger problem? What if we were to learn to live together in peace? If we can let the idea that Jesus taught take hold of our lives, do you realize what a great experience we could have? Religion is not to prepare us for death. Religion is to prepare us to live in God's world today.

Several years ago I saw a well-produced play about Adam and Eve. Adam was pictured as an obnoxious, arrogant person, totally insensitive to Eve. Adam took the prerogative of naming all the animals, and named himself ruler of everything. In the play's last scene, as the light dimmed, the actor portraying Adam came out on a bare stage and sat on a stool. In a very somber voice, he said, "Eve died last night and now I am outside of the Garden and I am alone." He briefly recounted his experiences; he told who he was and what had happened to him. Now, he said, "I have come to realize that wherever Eve was, was Eden," and the curtain fell.

Adam was right. Today, as you sit outside a hospital room in which a loved one is critically ill, you are terrified. None of the reports is good, and you continue your vigil. Then suddenly you sense the presence of God, you feel a harmony, and you say, "O God, I guess things are going to be all right either way, because my loved one seems to be comfortable, to have a sense of peace, and I know we will lose each other some day." You are not being hypothetical; you are facing facts.

What makes a situation like that all right? It is neither the hospital nor the threat of death. It is the fact that we feel God is with us. That's a real relationship. We all make mistakes, we all say the wrong things, and a relationship is broken. Losing someone very close to us is the most painful thing in the world, whether the loss is caused by death or relocation or a broken relationship. We really want an Eden. We may think of it as a specific job, a certain geographical location, or perhaps even an amount of money, but one day a realization flashes across our minds and we know what Eden is—it is a relationship.

You and I are so privileged to live in this world that God has given us. Yet, we make a hell of it. This is not done because we are bad, but because sometimes we just don't know enough, or we are not wise enough, or we haven't grown enough. God knows that, and he is here with us. I think God invites us to come back into the Garden, because he never put us out in the first place. When we were expelled, we thought he did it, although we really did it ourselves. We were trying to learn, to grow. God doesn't condemn us for that, because he wants us to learn, to ask questions, and to be. God invites us to come back into the Garden, and here we are. This is our world; what are we going to do with it? I think perhaps we can make it a Garden of Eden by restoring relationships. That's really what it is all about. Our problems are not God's punishments. God is not against us. Our punishments are what we do to ourselves and each other. We have never understood our loving heavenly Father, have we? Let us not blame ourselves, because we miss the whole point if we do. Instead, let us accept responsibility.

God asked, "Adam, Eve, what have you done?" They could have said, "Well, Lord, at times we have not done very well at all, but, O God, we want to be closer to you and closer to each other." Jesus spent his life talking about that idea, teaching in a way that calls us to God, urging us to make an Eden of God's world.

Come, join the family.